THE GRIEF TRAIN

A HEALING JOURNEY OF LOVE, LOSS AND RENEWAL

D1602252

MARINDA FREEMAN

Blessings,
Marinda

Black Rose Writing | Texas

The author grants the final approval for this literary material.

First printing

This book is a memoir. It reflects the author's present recollections of experiences over time. Some names and characteristics have been changed, some events have been compressed, and some dialogue has been recreated.

ISBN: 978-1-68433-536-7
PUBLISHED BY BLACK ROSE WRITING
www.blackrosewriting.com

Printed in the United States of America
Suggested Retail Price (SRP) $16.95

The Grief Train is printed in Sabon

*As a planet-friendly publisher, Black Rose Writing does its best to eliminate unnecessary waste to reduce paper usage and energy costs, while never compromising the reading experience. As a result, the final word count vs. page count may not meet common expectations.

Praise for

THE GRIEF TRAIN

A HEALING JOURNEY OF LOVE, LOSS AND RENEWAL

"Anyone who has lost the love of their life will identify with Marinda's story. Her openness and candor help the reader feel understood and know that they are not alone. This is also a narrative of hope and healing that can inspire any person navigating their own grief journey. I couldn't put the book down."

~Laurie Laychak-Chareq, widow of David Laychak killed at the Pentagon on September 11, 2001. TAPS (Tragedy Assistance Program for Survivors) Peer Mentor and Care Group Facilitator.

"An extraordinary book about grief . . . Marinda Freeman's journey through grief after the death of her beloved husband is indeed like a train. It goes through tunnels, bridges rough waters, and has a lot of unexpected curves, which is so very representative of most peoples' experience of the aftermath of losing a loved one. It's a great read."

~Sara Zeff Geber, PhD

Author, Essential Retirement Planning for Solo Agers

"There is no one 'right way' to grieve, and each of us in the grieving process will find words of wisdom, compassion, and resilience in Marinda's book. *The Grief Train*...covers much territory in the difficult field of coming to terms with a heart-breaking loss."

~Daphne Crocker White, PhD

Clinical Psychologist and poet,

Board of Directors California Institute of Integral Studies

"*The Grief Train* is an invitation into the author's world, to sit at her kitchen counter and chat about her magical miracle love story with her husband Mike, as well as her journey after his passing. She shares her heart, her experiences and her memories. I loved reading this precious book and I know it will help many people."

~Susan Fox, DACM, L.Ac., FABORM

To Gayle and Wayne without whom I would not have met and married the love of my life, and thus, this story would not have happened.

THE GRIEF TRAIN

A HEALING JOURNEY OF LOVE, LOSS AND RENEWAL

Table of Contents

Introduction

About Me

I became a widow on October 21, 2009 when my husband died suddenly of a massive heart attack. He was fifty-seven years old. We had been married less than five years with so much ahead of us. "Widow" is such a strange word. When I learned Mike had died, I thought, "I've never been a widow before" – a new experience to add to my life. I had no idea that this experience would be a journey of over five years.

Why did I start writing?

It was suggested to me that I start a blog about being a widow after Mike died, that it might be a good way to process the experience – and to observe my thoughts and feelings. I'd never written a blog before, although I have done a lot of writing in my career.

After a year and a half of writing, I started to share what I had written with others that had experienced the loss of a husband, a wife or a sibling. They each told me that reading my blog posts had helped them. Here is a touching example:

Marinda,

Thank you for sharing such honest deep thoughts and emotions. I have enjoyed reading your entries. Everyone grieves for as long as it takes and maybe the rest of their life. There is no magic pill for healing. I have found learning to manage the pain is the best I can do at times.

Some experiences have a profound impact on our souls. How wonderful you met your soul mate and danced through life together, if even for a short time. It is rare that we have such beautiful experiences with another physical being on earth. Mike understood you and your challenges. He supported you 100% and loved you unconditionally. This is what we grieve, the unconditional love that person had for us. So hard to find from mere mortals. So hard to replace. Keep sharing, as it is beautiful to read about the window into your soul.

Love, P.M.

After more time went by, I took a writing class and got feedback that I should turn this into a book – again to share with others going through the process of loss. And it is a process.

This book is organized chronologically by the progression of time as I went through my journey after Mike died. I invite you to dip in anywhere that might be helpful to where you are at this moment or start at the beginning and read straight through. This is not a how-to book, rather more a meditation and noticing of the thoughts and feelings that arose as I moved through my grief and mourning. I hope this book will help you recognize and navigate the emotions and reflections you may be going through. May this book be a companion on your healing journey.

When We Mourn

In the Op-Ed section of the New York Times, there was an article* I tore out so I could read it again. You never know when something sparks an emotion, a thought, a piece of the puzzle that you didn't know was missing. Here's the quote that had me pondering:

"When we mourn, isn't it not just for our relationship with a person, but also for the physical presence of her, of her aliveness? The voice, smell, textures and warmth, the gestures we know intimately, these are replaced with their opposites in death. We are left with a hole that the energy that powered the person through life once filled."

That last sentence nails it. "We are left with a hole that the energy that powered the person through life once filled." That's why I felt empty, at a loss – a loss of presence, of energy, of aliveness – when Mike suddenly departed. Yes, with all the mannerisms, habits and behaviors that I loved or drove me crazy but with him gone, I missed them all.

When Mike passed on to the "next expression of life," I knew he was and is fine. I am the one left to adjust to the change – to learn how to live with that hole that suddenly appeared, and to first feel the feelings of loss, of sadness, of whatever I am feeling. Feeling my feelings was not a practice I learned growing up or during most of my life. I was more focused on action, doing and thinking. In the last ten to fifteen years, I have learned more about feeling my feelings – to even being aware of what my feelings are rather than what I think.

In every experience, I know there is a gift. Some call it a silver lining. Mike's death gave me the gift of learning to really accept my feelings, to dive down deep into them, and to be present with my feelings – to allow them. Our society doesn't always encourage us to stop and feel our feelings. We have to move on. What's next? Keep on keeping on, rather than stopping – to pause and ask, what am I feeling now? Sometimes, especially in the first two to three years, feelings of grief would come like a wave that crashed over me and I would be overcome with the grief and sadness. Only after developing a practice of diving into the waves of my feelings, could I discover how to collect the energy, the aliveness that was Mike and bring it into my heart to fill that hole. What I have learned is that this process happens over time. It's not a quick fix. Years, it takes years–and that's ok.

*The New York Times, *Sunday, November 2, 2014*

Wild Messengers, by Jennifer S. Holland

A National Geographic contributor, and the author most recently, of
Unlikely Heroes: 37 Inspiring Stories of Courage and Heart
This is an essay from Menagerie, a series about our relationship to animals, at nytimes.com/opinionator

Chapter One
The Grief Train Arrives

What Happened

Thursday, October 22, 2009

Mike was working in Southern California during the week, flying home on Thursday evenings for the weekend. It was Thursday. The plan was to pick him up at the airport that evening, as usual. In the afternoon during a business meeting, I received a call from his boss asking me if Mike was there (at home in Marin County). I told him no; he wasn't. He said that Mike had not been at work yesterday or again today. He would go to Mike's apartment and would call me back. I felt my stomach drop, my heart was pounding – something was wrong, and I didn't know what.

After my meeting, I left a message for Mike on his cell phone and headed to the Oakland airport. I waited in the parking lot by Walmart just outside the airport as I had done so many times before, expecting Mike's call when he landed as the signal to drive to the airport and pick him up outside Southwest baggage claim. I didn't get a call from Mike. So I drove to the airport, parked and went inside to see about his flight. I still hadn't heard from Mike's boss. I discovered the flight had arrived, but no Mike. Oh, dear. Something was not right. While inside the terminal, I received a call on my cell phone from a sheriff in Orange County, CA asking me to call him back on a land line. He said he couldn't talk to me on my cell.

Now I was really getting anxious and panicked. I asked someone about a phone booth and was directed to one near baggage claim. I called the Sheriff back. The first question he asked me, "Was Mike on any drugs or medication?" I told the officer he was taking medication to help him stop smoking. He then told me that Mike had died. It appeared to be a heart attack and that the coroner would call me back later with an autopsy report. I was stunned. I staggered back to my car and called my best friend, Kay, to tell her. "No, that can't be Mike you are talking about," she said. She didn't understand what I was saying and couldn't believe the news. Me neither. He was young, only fifty-seven. How could this be? It was hard to absorb this news. It felt like my ears were ringing. My body felt like it was in a distorting mirror – vibrating back and forth between fat and thin, or rather in this reality and not in this reality.

I called my daughter to tell her the news and let her know I was driving home from the airport. Looking back, I realized I was in shock. I was on automatic pilot on the drive home, having driven it so many times before. Leaving the Oakland airport, I drove up Highway 980 to 580 and over the Richmond-San Rafael Bridge back to Marin County.

On the way home, I stopped in San Rafael at a workshop I was supposed be attending to support my dear friend and minister, Katherine. I interrupted the workshop for a moment to talk privately with Katherine and told her about Mike. I felt like I was a robot reporting the news. When I arrived home, my daughter and my friend and neighbor, Diana, were there to meet me. I sat down and started shaking. I felt like I had been in an accident. I called

Mike's sister in Vancouver to tell her. She couldn't believe what I was telling her. I also called several other good friends of ours to tell them the news. I got a call back from friends in Hawaii, letting me know that Marjorie, one of our friends who is a medium, said she connected with Mike and that he was totally surprised that he had left his body and died. She said that it was like he was sitting on the couch eating popcorn and then poof; he was gone. In some strange way, knowing that Mike was as surprised as we all were was comforting to me.

Eventually, that evening, I received a call from the coroner. She explained that Mike had had a massive heart attack. He was sitting on the couch and it had happened the morning before, on Wednesday, around 7:00 am. This explained why Mike had not been at work Wednesday or Thursday.

More of the Story

I finally heard from Mike's boss. He explained that the sheriff asked him to not call me as the sheriff needed to make the call to me. I'm not sure why, but that's what transpired. He then explained what happened at his end. Mike had not come to work on Wednesday. When Mike didn't come to work on Thursday, Mike's boss called Mike – no answer. He called me as I mentioned, and I confirmed Mike was not here at home. He then went over to Mike's apartment and found Mike's car in the garage and the door to the apartment locked from the inside. He called the police. When they arrived, Mike's boss explained that the apartment was a company apartment, and he explained how Mike's car was in the garage and the door was locked from the inside. He gave the police permission to break open the door. Instead, they called the fire department who attempted to get in through a window, but it was too high for them to access it. Finally, after many hours had passed, they broke down the door–and found Mike on the couch.

Katherine arrived after all the calls and just sat with me for a while that evening. It was so helpful to have someone to share and review all this overwhelming information. I don't know how I got to sleep that night, but I did.

Carrying On

I woke up the next morning feeling numb and not sure how I would get my work done for my event design business. There were three big events to produce in the next two weeks. I had to put my mourning aside and do the event work required. I could only think about the next two weeks. The phone was ringing like crazy, so I called my sister-in-law and another friend, Brooke, and asked them to come over and help handle the calls. They both arrived very soon.

As my friends handled the ringing phones, I took a few minutes in the afternoon to go upstairs to my bedroom and call my friend Sara. Sitting on the couch in our bedroom, I told Sara about Mike and asked her when I could schedule a session with her. Sara is a medium, and I have had readings from her in the past. I knew she could give me insight and information about Mike. I needed to know what happened to Mike, to connect with him again and find out how he was doing with this big change. I asked Sara how long it would take for Mike to be acclimated to his new "place" and thus be available for the reading. She said about one month. I knew that it was a shock to him, since my friend, Marjorie, in Hawaii had mentioned this, and said it would take some time for him to "land."

Sara told me while I was on the phone with her Mike was there, lying on the bed just a few feet away in our bedroom. She said Mike told her he was really sorry he left me and he had been very surprised at his quick departure. I was in such shock during this call that I didn't have much to say or know how to respond to Mike's comments or his "presence" in the bedroom.

I now had to put all that aside as I headed back downstairs. So many calls were coming in AND I had to work. Looking back, I'm amazed that I accomplished all that needed to be done in these two weeks. I had several other friends jump in to help me finish the logistics and details for these three events. At the same time, there were arrangements to be made about Mike. The coroner had asked if I wanted the body shipped up here to Northern CA. I did not need to see the body. I knew that wasn't him anymore. He was gone. The body was just an empty shell. Having attended other funerals with a viewing of the body, I recognized that the deceased was not there. It wasn't them anymore without their aliveness. I didn't need to see Mike's body; I knew what that looked like – with him in it. Katherine helped me find a funeral home in Orange County to have his body sent from the morgue to be cremated. I decided when to go down to Southern

California and clean out Mike's apartment and set dates for the memorials – one soon in Orange County for those he worked with, and another in mid-December here in Marin for friends and relatives.

To add another layer of complexity and challenge, the largest event I was coordinating during these two weeks was on Treasure Island (between San Francisco and Oakland). Just a few days before this gala event, a cable broke on the Oakland Bay Bridge and they closed the bridge. There was only one access over the Bridge to Treasure Island from San Francisco. I drove over the Golden Gate Bridge, through the city on to the bridge to Treasure Island. The first day I was there for setup and the next day for the evening event. It was eerie driving across the bridge with absolutely no cars on it. All five lanes, usually filled with hundreds, thousands of cars, were empty. It was definitely one of the very few "Acts of God" that I have ever had in over 30 years of producing events. I wanted to stop and take pictures. It was an image I will never forget. I felt I had entered an alternate universe.

This empty bridge reflected my life at this time. I was working like usual, and another part of me was empty, like the bridge – in an alternate universe with Mike no longer in my life. I could not have made it through those two weeks – and beyond – without the help and support of my friends.

After my three events were over, I flew down to Orange County with my friend, Diana, and we cleaned out Mike's apartment, packed up what to bring with us in his car, determined what to ship and what I could donate. A woman I had contacted met us at the apartment with boxes and helped take away the donated items and ship other boxes to me. Diana and I stopped by and looked at the golf club recommended for Mike's Memorial on November 19th and I booked the space. The last stop on the way north from Orange County was to pick up Mike's ashes. We stopped at the funeral home; I signed some papers, and they handed me a gray shopping bag with a dark gray box inside. The box just fit in the bag, so I could only see the top of the box. It was way heavier than I expected. I put it on the back seat, and we drove back to Marin County in Mike's beloved Mini Cooper. When we got home, I put the bag with his ashes on a shelf in my closet, tucked under hanging clothes. I did not want to look at it or examine the box.

Our Story

Mike and I had met briefly in 2002 at the wedding of the daughter of mutual friends. I was the wedding planner. I remember seeing Mike enter the hotel lobby, but I did not remember that he sat at my table, as I was up and down constantly while managing the reception. We were re-introduced at a brunch in May 2004 at the home of the same mutual friends, Wayne and Gayle, in Sausalito.

Mike called me a month later and said he had a business proposal. "I have to do an internship to complete my degree at the California Culinary Academy. Would you consider having me come work for you for three months, five days a week, and you don't have to pay me?" How could I say no? "Yes!", I said. I had several big events coming up in September, so I welcomed the help. Mike had taken a sabbatical from his thirty-year career and had moved to Marin and was attending the Culinary Academy in San Francisco to get a degree as a Cordon Bleu Chef because he always liked to cook.

I drove around to appointments that summer saying to myself, "I have a lovely man in my house, a British gentleman. This must be an indication that men are coming into my life." Working together, we got to know each other. We had dinner together a few times, and he got to know my daughter, Esther.

Mike and I found we had many things in common. We both shared a love of the Beatles. We had seen them live – me in Chicago twice, he in Liverpool and London. We both loved to cook and loved good food. We both had been to boarding school. We both had been young when our mothers died – he at sixteen, me at ten. I'd lived a few places in the U.S., traveled to Europe and lived in Tokyo. He had visited and/or lived in forty-nine countries. What amazing stories he had!

We got through my major event in September, a weekend Chocolate Festival benefitting a nonprofit for thousands at Ghirardelli Square, which ended Mike's internship. Mike graduated from the California Culinary Academy in October. He invited me to the graduation along with his sister and her husband, who came down from Vancouver, BC. I felt honored to be there.

Over the Thanksgiving weekend, Mike was visited by Immigration authorities and was arrested. Turns out he was on a student visa while attending the Culinary Academy and he had not renewed his visa after he finished school. Two of his friends lobbied to get him out of jail and paid his bail. Mike then hired a lawyer to assist him with this situation.

The beginning of December, Mike joined me at my friend, Kim's, annual holiday sale. He took Kim aside and asked if he had a chance with me. She told him, "Go for it!" Shortly thereafter we went on our first date, out to a special local restaurant for a wonderful dinner. For our second date, Mike invited me to his apartment for dinner. The first course was lobster bisque. I had one taste and the words, "Will you marry me?" went through my head, followed with, "I can't say that!" The lobster bisque was divine. I don't remember what the entrée was, although I'm sure it was also delicious. And so we began seeing each other.

Mike had meetings with the attorney and a court date was set for early January regarding his visa status. At court, it was determined that he had to leave the U.S. by May 1st and had to be out of the country for a year. He could then come back into the States.

In March 2005, Mike asked me to marry him, and asked me to try on his mother's diamond solitaire. He had told me before the story of his mum's ring and that he had been carrying it around the world with him for over twenty-five years. Mike had never married. Living all over the world didn't allow a lot of time for dating. The ring fit. "It's like the glahss slippah!" said Mike in his beautiful English accent.

A couple weeks later, Mike called me and said that the attorney told him we should get married right away. I was just walking into the offices of the spiritual community I attended, so I asked the minister when she was available next week to officiate at a wedding. She said next Wednesday was good. So, Wednesday, April 6th was the date. Being an event and wedding planner, I made a few calls and had everything set for the next week. I talked to my brother and sister-in-law, Hunter and Leslie, and they generously offered their home. I booked a caterer and got a wedding cake donated from the baker I was working with for a client special birthday celebration event coming up. My favorite musicians, Karen and John, were available, and I made calls to friends inviting them to attend. We had twenty-four family and friends present. It was a lovely day. I wore an olive silk Eileen Fisher suit with a cream silk tank and pearls borrowed from a friend. Mike's best man was Wayne. My sister, Elizabeth, was my maid of honor. There were boutonnieres for the men and bouquets for Elizabeth and me. Unbeknownst to me until the memorial – and really not until I watched the video afterwards – did I realize that Wayne and his wife, Gayle, had had the intention to bring Mike and me together since their daughter's wedding. I am more grateful to them than they know for bringing Mike into my life.

Getting married did not change the situation that Mike had to leave the country. So, on May 1st, he headed to Vancouver, BC in his Mini to stay with his sister and her husband. I visited Mike several times there. He then got a job in Calgary, so I visited him there. My daughter also joined me for some of these visits.

I had been planning a remodel of my house for about five years, working with an architect on different options for the remodel and the addition of a second-floor master bedroom suite. It seemed like I had been calling in a relationship with the plans for a new master bedroom. Mike and I pored over the house plans together and made some changes to the master bedroom to accommodate his bedroom suite of furniture. We also reviewed the kitchen plans – anticipating two chefs in the kitchen. Mike and I shopped for the kitchen equipment together. We couldn't pass up the Wolf double oven, or a wine refrigerator. So, while Mike was away in Canada and my daughter was in boarding school for high school, my house became a construction site and I lived in the front three bedrooms of the house (one room being my office) while the rest of the house was torn apart. Mike's furniture and most of mine was put in storage. It was exciting for me to see the manifestation of many years of planning coming to fruition. When the house was finished, I had help to combine our furniture and moving everything that would fit into our new home. It was a great way to start a new marriage.

Finally, a year passed, and Mike could come home. Then came the appointments with the U.S. Immigration Service in San Francisco. We had to provide letters from friends and other documentation that proved we were married because we loved each other, not as a convenience so Mike could be in this country. One of the most important documents turned out to be our wedding announcement and story I sent out to all our friends after we were married. I had written the story of our meeting and had my friend and graphic designer set it up so it looked like a Vows column from the New York Times. I always loved reading the Vows column and thought our story was worthy of being one of their articles. Obviously, I didn't mention to the Immigration officer that this was not really in the New York Times. After several meetings, Mike's status was approved with me as his sponsor. Hurray!

Mike found work with a company he had worked for previously in Texas and was working for in Calgary – the Fluor Corporation. Their west coast offices were in Orange County, CA so he started commuting down there four days a week. He liked the work. It was a bit different from managing a project on site. As he had so much experience, the new management position utilized his expertise and offered new things for him to learn.

Mike and I finally took our honeymoon to Hawaii in August 2006 – a year plus after our wedding. Mike had a vision of retiring to Hawaii and opening a restaurant. We stayed at Kona Village for part of the time and also spent time at the home of close friends. We had a wonderful time.

Mike and I were both passionate about cooking and loved doing so in our remodeled kitchen. Over the years, we hosted many dinner parties with Mike usually making the entrée and I would make the salad and dessert. They didn't do much with salad greens in the UK when Mike was growing up. Mike made an amazing lamb curry with all the condiments. My brother loved his Spaghetti Bolognese. And, of course, all our friends raved about his lobster bisque. Mike was also famous for his scrambled eggs. My daughter makes them now, so they live on.

Mike was a very generous and thoughtful man. He surprised me each Valentines' Day with a special gift. One year it was a beautiful nightgown and robe. Another year it was a pair of diamond earrings because he had noticed that I didn't have any and thought I should. I'd never had a man give me gifts for Valentine's Day with such thought and care. Mike stepped into a new role of stepfather. Not that it was easy for him or my daughter to start with, but he and my daughter ended up getting along well. I think they were more alike than I was like either of them. I so appreciated his love, caring and support of my daughter.

Mike was famous for his scrambled eggs. My daughter, Esther, learned to make them so she is carrying on Mike's scrambled eggs recipe.

Mike's Scrambled Eggs

For every egg, add one Tbsp milk (you can replace with unsweetened almond or coconut milk, if preferred).

Whisk eggs together in a bowl.

Heat a little butter in a frying pan on low heat.

Pour eggs into pan. Stirring constantly let the eggs start to heat up then take the pan on and off the heat. Continue doing this until the eggs are cooked through. They will be very creamy because you are cooking them slowly – stirring constantly.

Serve with toast. Bacon is always good.

The OC (Orange County) Memorial

Because Mike had worked with many of the people in his company and in the industry for twenty-five years or more, I felt it was important to have a memorial near the office so they could come and have closure with Mike's passing. I also wanted to make sure both memorials were recorded for Mike's family in Vancouver, BC and England. I wasn't sure if his sisters would be coming to the memorial in December.

I confirmed a location for Mike's Memorial in Marin County for mid-December at a wonderful restaurant on the water in their private room upstairs. I had started working with Katherine to design the memorial program. In this process, I collected Mike's story – where he was born, where he lived, and included stories he told me.

With Mike's story put together, I used that to design the Memorial program for Mike's fellow employees and business friends. Just two weeks after being down in Orange County to clear out his apartment and book the space, I flew down again to Orange County on November 19th with my friend, Margaret. I really appreciated her coming with me so I didn't have to do this alone.

We arrived at the golf clubhouse to review the setup, sound system and flowers I had ordered. I also connected with the videographer I had booked to record the program so I could share it with Mike's family. As guests arrived, I greeted and welcomed them. To start the memorial program, I opened with a prayer and then talked about Mike.

"Mike's life was a fascinating story. I kept telling him to write it all down. He didn't, and I wasn't taking notes. So some dates may not be 100% accurate.

"Mike was born in Egypt. Mike's dad was a Suez Canal pilot. He spent his first years in Egypt with his parents and sister, Cecelie, who is a year older than Mike. His two older sisters were away at boarding school in England. When Mike was five, they had to leave Egypt quickly because of the Suez Crisis, leaving most of their things behind. Mike said he had a vivid memory of standing at the bottom of a huge gangplank wearing short pants and carrying his suitcase – ready to board the ship for England.

"At age seven, Mike started boarding school in England at Stonyhurst, a Jesuit boarding school, not too far from his parents' home near Liverpool, England. Stonyhurst is the Catholic equivalent of Eton. The buildings at the school date back to the 1200's. As a youth he sang in the choir, and when he went to Liverpool College at age thirteen, he became a competitive swimmer and rugby champion, playing for Cheshire, the county he lived in.

"Mike's father moved to Bahrain as Harbour Master, and as a Naval Architect oversaw the building of the new harbor for Bahrain. Mike and Cecelie went there for the summer holidays. In 1966, Mike's father and mother moved to Nigeria and Mike and Cecelie visited them there during the summer months.

"Mike learned to cook as a child from his mum and loved to cook and entertain his friends – wherever he lived. In 1981, Mike emigrated to Canada and became a Canadian citizen while still remaining a British citizen.

"Mike's career in the engineering and construction industry spanned thirty-plus years. He worked for Phillips Petroleum, Shell and Fluor Corporation. He lived in many places, managing multi-billion-dollar construction projects – from the wilds of Northwest Scotland to the beaches of Thailand, from Venezuela to Saudi Arabia, and from Calgary to Houston. All this traveling, staying usually two to three years at a construction project location, didn't present Mike with many opportunities for dating and commitment, and so no marriage occurred for him. Three years in Saudi Arabia with no women did not add to his prospects. He declared that the availability of women makes a huge difference!

"Mike's life and career took him all over the world – to forty-nine countries. He had experiences that most of us have not had, including surviving many accidents. I think he had many lives like a cat. He got off a plane before it crashed on the next leg. He survived a train crash, a boat sinking, and a helicopter crash into the water – where one of the passengers refused, at least initially, to take off his brand new Lucchesi cowboy boots and get in the lifeboat. Earlier, when Mike was fifteen, visiting his parents in Lagos, Nigeria one summer, he was shot at while racing home in a car with friends through the city after curfew. Fortunately, they made it.

"Using his years of experience, in 2000, Mike and a friend created a project management software program for the Engineering & Construction industry. A few sales were made to big companies and then in 2003 the dot-com bubble burst and people stopped buying software. So Mike decided to take a sabbatical and moved to Marin County to be near friends. He enrolled in the California Culinary Academy in San Francisco for the eighteen-month course to become a Cordon Bleu Chef. Which is how we met – being introduced by mutual friends."

Next, I invited the guests to come up to the front of the room and say something, if they would like. Many came up and spoke about Mike, their relationships with him, what an expert he was at his job, as well as the kindness he showed to them and others. Some mentioned that Mike was so well respected in the business and the industry. He also showed so much heart and care for those he was managing. Those that could not attend were represented by having their comments read by mutual friends of Mike's. I closed the program by thanking everyone that came and invited them to stay and enjoy refreshments.

It was such a pleasure to meet so many people that Mike worked with. Everyone said over and over that they were so grateful to have come.

Margaret and I flew home that evening. Now just one memorial to go.

Clearing the Closet

The first few weeks after Mike's death, I was too numb to feel much when I stepped into our closet. Our. I so miss that. It's a walk-in closet that had Mike's clothes on one side, mine on the other. Once I was past the events and the first memorial, I started to become more aware of what was hanging on Mike's side of the closet. Walking into the closet each day and inhaling his presence lingering in his clothes was a reminder he was no longer here.

I have always had an altar in my bedroom – a place for sacred objects. I set it up on the beautiful many-drawer chest with a carved Ganesha I had given Mike and a carved Buddha – both bought in Bali. There was a crystal cluster Mike had given me, my crystal ball, candles and flowers. Now I added Mike to the altar with pictures from our wedding, a picture of Mike with his sisters, the little metal heart he carried in his pocket and a few other things of his. For me, it was a way of honoring and remembering him, and a place to acknowledge his presence in my life and a way to focus my awareness of this change.

Having to decide what to do with his clothes was another step in confronting the reality that he was now gone. A couple weeks after the memorial in Orange County, I was finally ready to spend the weekend sorting and packing up Mike's clothes. I would touch and look at his much-loved collection of Tommy Bahama short-sleeve silk Hawaiian shirts hanging on the rod and remember how much he wanted to retire to Hawaii. I would wish he was still here to wear them. Or conversely, I would wonder what I was going to do with them. I didn't want to just donate all his things to a nonprofit. They were too big for me. Mike was a big guy. About 5'11" and muscular. Like a football player. He was a rugby champion in school and a swimmer. He was as thick through the chest (from front to back) as I was wide (from side to side). When I would lie down next to Mike, he on his back, me on my side, I would marvel at this.

The boxes of suits and clothes I had packed up and sent from his Orange County apartment had been sitting in my dining room for several weeks. I decided to take the clothes to a local organization that provides clothing for men and women, so they have the right clothes for job interviews, giving them greater confidence. I sorted through the boxes sent from his apartment first, putting the suits and dress shirts in bags. Going through the boxes was easier as these things had already been sorted and packed.

I called my friend, Kay, and asked if she wanted some of Mike's uniform black long sleeve knit shirts. When Kay was here in December for the memorial, I gave her the knit shirts and Mike's favorite black leather jacket I had saved for her. It felt good to have a friend wearing some of Mike's favorite clothes and she loves wearing them.

I set aside Mike's really nice Tommy Bahama casual shirts and some sweaters to share with his friends. We have a wonderful group of friends that get together for a potluck dinner about once a month. At the next gathering, I put out Mike's clothes and let the men choose what they wanted. The shirts got snapped up. Each one came out beaming and modeling a shirt. Rick put on the cream wool Aryan sweater. He loved it! They were all thrilled to have something of Mike's, and I was happy that I could share Mike with them in this way.

Mike had a lot of style – one of the things I so liked about him. I still think about his black leather dress shoes. They weren't patent leather, but they had a shine to them, with a thin sole. Elegant. When he was all dressed up in a suit and those shoes – wow. I had never known a man with dress shoes like these. The shoes were like the "bing" that set off his whole ensemble. Must have been the British in him – having the right accessories for formal affairs. I was so sad remembering him all dressed up – as I wouldn't see that again. I got a knot in my stomach just thinking about this. Holding onto his shoes seemed sort of crazy. What would I do with them?

I went through the closet shelf by shelf, drawer by drawer, and everything on hangers, packing the clothes in large shopping bags. I kept an olive cotton sweater I had given him that matched his eyes. We both have green eyes. It's oversized but great to wear with jeans. I also kept a couple shirts, including a beautiful black linen shirt. A couple years later, however, I ended up sending it to Kay as I stopped wearing much black. Not because of mourning, but because with my hair now more gray than blonde, gray looks better than black on me now. I used to wear a lot of black. When Mike would come home, he would put on his uniform – black casual knit pants and a black long-sleeve or short-sleeve T-shirt, depending on the weather. Many times, we looked like twins – in dress only. Here's a picture with our friends, Wayne and Gayle, with Mike and me in black shirts and jeans/jean skirt.

Mike had some beautiful sarongs that he bought when he lived in Thailand. When we were in meditation circle, he would change from his jeans to a sarong. He preferred wearing one – it was more comfortable; he said. I kept all his sarongs and added them to the stack of sarongs I had collected over the years.

I cleaned out the closet of Mike's clothes and accessories. My dining room was filled with many bags. My friend, Brooke, agreed to take the bags to the nonprofit. I have to admit that's as far as I went. I didn't clean out the drawers with Mike's toiletries in the bathroom or the drawers in the chest on his side of the bed. It took me a couple years before I cleaned out the bathroom drawers and about four years before I finally tackled the drawers in the bedside table. There wasn't even that much in those bedside drawers, but they were just as Mike had left them. I would open them every so often and look at what was in there and close the drawers again. What took me so long? I wasn't ready to say goodbye to everything, I guess.

After all I had completed the sorting on Sunday afternoon, I had a snack. I sliced up a pear and ended up slicing the very tip of my little finger off – just the skin. However, now there was a hole, and it was bleeding. I called my friend, Katherine, and told her I needed to go to the emergency room. She offered to take me. We had set an appointment for that afternoon to discuss plans for Mike's memorial scheduled for December 13th. We discussed ideas for the memorial while we sat in the emergency waiting room for two hours – with me holding my finger in a towel above my head. Eventually, I was bandaged with some "fake" skin and the finger was wrapped up. I found out later that the little finger is connected to the heart. Seems applicable as Mike had a heart attack and my heart was broken with the loss. It was a reminder to me that I wasn't doing as well as I thought I was and that I was more affected by Mike's death than I may have admitted to myself.

A similar experience happened to me three years later when my sister ended up in the hospital in the ICU. I almost sliced the end of my left forefinger off cutting vegetables and had to go to the emergency room again. I learned later that this finger is connected to the lungs. My sister was having trouble breathing and ended up dying from pneumonia. I've been cooking since I was young, so I think there was more to it than just sloppy knife work. It seems to me there was an emotional connection to these two "accidents." I was more emotionally affected by the situations with Mike's death and my sister dying than I was conscious of – or acknowledged – and it showed up in a very physical way. Hello! Maybe it was also reminding me how connected I was to each of them.

Checking in with Mike

Almost exactly a month after Mike died, I had my scheduled session with Sara. At my very first session with Sara years ago, I didn't know what to expect. Sara and I were at a women's retreat. We took a walk in the woods and found some rocks to sit on. As a medium, Sara is able to connect beyond the veil and communicate with those that have died. She started talking and telling those I could not see that they needed to take turns speaking. There was a crowd of people wanting to come through. My paternal grandmother seemed to be first in line. Sara told me what they said. My grandmother was encouraging me to write about our family history and to include the photos and letters I have that were handed down by women in my family over the past one-hundred-fifty-plus years. (I haven't done this project yet, but it's on my list and I promise to do so, Grandma!) There were a few other family members that came through, my mother being one of them. She has come through in other readings, too. She has been watching over me since she died when I was ten. I learned this for the first time in the early 70s when I went to the Berkeley Psychic Institute and had a student reading.

A few years before Mike's passing, I had suggested that he and I have a reading with Sara over the phone about a month after his brother-in-law, Jon, committed suicide. It was such a shock to everyone, as there had been no warning that something was going on or that he was emotionally in trouble. Mike wanted to know what happened and how he was doing, and perhaps share the information with his sister, Jon's wife. Jon explained he had not been feeling like he could go on any longer. He said it had nothing to do with his relationship with his wife or with anyone else. Such a shame. So sad. It was helpful to hear his explanation as we had no idea what had happened. At least it filled in the blanks a bit. He seemed to be in a better place.

In the 90s I read the *Celestine Prophecy* and other books in the series by James Redfield. Maybe you read these books, too? The last book, <u>The Twelfth Insight</u> (published in 2011), gave me a sense of understanding the world beyond the veil which seems to be just outside our reach because it is invisible to us. Sometimes in stories, such as the one in this book, it is easier to understand what a situation would feel like – rather than just being given information. To become aware of those that have gone on beyond this physical experience is not something I am able to do, but I have met and had readings from several people that can do this. These beings outside our physical dimension – our friends and relatives – are very much awake and aware. When we think of them, they can show up or be around us, even though we may not realize it. Recently, my friend, Diana, had a reading with a medium about her father who died about six months prior. Through the medium, her father said he was sitting on a bench having the best time talking to people he hadn't seen in ages. She said she had to laugh – it was so like her dad. He loved to chat with friends.

So, I was on the phone with Sara at our appointed time. I called her from the couch again in my bedroom, with a notebook and pen to take notes. I was looking forward to this session, to give me some sense of what happened and how Mike is doing. Mike was right there with Sara when we started the session. Actually, Sara said he had been hanging around her all morning waiting for the session. The first thing she said is that his love is palpable – he loves me, always loves me. It was a happy and sad moment to hear that from Mike. Both Sara and I were crying. Sara described Mike's energy as a quiet nature, a quiet presence with lots of love. She felt his mass – quiet but stocky. Mike was a big guy. Seems like he still is.

Mike offered to tell me what happened. I wasn't that interested as he was already gone, but he proceeded through Sara, to explain that he had not felt well and had been up all night. He thought it was the flu or something and was totally surprised that he left his body in the morning. Sara asked, "Why didn't you take yourself to the hospital, you dodo?" He had no answer to that.

Mike said he is in a beautiful place with rolling green hills. Very peaceful. He mostly wanted to spend the time of our session addressing what I was going to do after the December 13th memorial. After the second memorial, I didn't want to do anything. I would be ready to stop. Mike insisted that I make a list of ten things I would do after the memorial. He was quite bossy about making a list and having me be accountable. This was not really how he acted when he was in his body! So, I made a list of ten things. I don't know where that list is now, but the one thing I did follow up on was writing a blog. That was one of Mike's suggestions and he urged me to make it happen. He wanted to focus on where I am going from here. He was being so pushy. Quite different from his usual, but this wasn't the usual.

Mike said that his love is constant for me and that love will never interrupt my feelings for someone else when that day comes. I missed Mike. I wished he was still here, and this was as close as I could get. He encouraged me to open up and find love again. He said that a lot of light comes out of me and he appreciated all the light I showed him. Mike acknowledged that he didn't take care of himself physically. This is true. He stopped smoking when we got married but then had started again, much to my disappointment. He had also gained weight and was not exercising. I had been worried about his health. Mike said from childhood he felt that he didn't count. This was so heartbreaking to hear that he carried this inner conversation, this feeling within him his whole life. I wish I had known.

Mike wanted me to know that I am here for a purpose – to help bring the world to a higher vibration – to take my light out in the world to teach others to do the same. There will be lots of joy and rewards for me over the next twenty-five to forty years. "Everyone thinks you are on the right path," Mike said. I didn't ask him who "everyone" is.

During this session, I felt our connection and tears streamed down my face. It was still so sad. I had such mixed feelings. It was good to know that Mike was well, filled with love and in a beautiful place – which I truly knew and expected to be the case. However, I was so sad and grieving that he was no longer here in my life. We had so many plans for what we wanted to do together. He wanted to retire to Hawaii and open up a restaurant. We wanted to go to Bali together. I wanted to show him New York City. None of our plans or ideas would happen now. It was more than disappointing. Sitting on the couch, I felt like I was a puddle of tears and sorrow. He was gone. It was hard to adjust to this new reality. No Mike. No more my rock. No more. After we had finally found each other. I was back to just me.

And at the same time . . . having the session with Sara confirmed for me that Love knows no boundaries of time or space.

December Memorial

By the middle of November, after the memorial for Mike's business associates, I had confirmed all the components for the December memorial. A videographer to record it. Katherine to lead the memorial. My talented musician friends, Karen and John. Mike's older sister, Moira, was flying down from Vancouver, BC. Mike's other sister, Cecelie, and her husband, Pete, were flying in from England. My cousins Whitney and Morgan would be there, too, with Whitney arriving from New York.

My friend and graphic designer, Anne, designed an invitation, and I emailed it out on November 17th to let friends and family know where and when the Memorial would be. I had booked the private room at Servino Ristorante in Tiburon – a beautiful private room upstairs with a view of boats and the bay. I chose the beverages and hors d'oeuvres to be passed after the ceremony.

Memorial Invitation

Here is the memorial invitation that was mailed out to family and friends.

AN HONORING AND CELEBRATION
OF THE LIFE OF
JAMES MICHAEL FARRELL

SUNDAY, DECEMBER 13, 2009

2:00 TO 5:00 PM

SERVINO RESTAURANT
9 MAIN STREET, TIBURON, CA

BRING YOUR STORIES AND REMEMBRANCES
TO SHARE.

PLEASE REPLY BY MONDAY, DECEMBER 7
TO MARINDA FREEMAN
415-924-9145 OR marinda@mfproductions.net

Many months before, I had bought tickets to see the
Broadway show, *Wicked*, in San Francisco at the beginning
of December. Now it was time to go with my daughter and
a friend. I didn't know that I would end up crying like
crazy when the song, "For Good," was sung. It touched my
heart with the truth of it in the refrain – "Who can say if
I've been changed for the better? But because I knew you,
I have been changed for good." And I knew at that moment
that this song had to be sung at Mike's memorial. The
Universe does provide exactly what is needed at the perfect
time. I contacted Karen to tell her about the song. She
didn't know it but agreed to learn it.

All the pieces were coming together for this event, Mike's memorial. Yes, this was another event, or a series of events leading up to the memorial and just after. In writing this book, I found the event timeline I created starting with December 8th when my friend, Kay, arrived to help and ended with her departure on December 16th. I must have been on automatic pilot. Clearly, I can do event planning and organization in my sleep or in a major fog of loss. I don't recall doing half the things that were on the timeline. Obviously, I did them as I was scheduled with many activities, including setting up a small private party for a client the day before the memorial.

The evening before the memorial, another ceremony, called a Black Earth Ceremony, was scheduled by friends of Mike's and mine. Our group of friends have gathered to do this ceremony before. It is from The Arica School, founded in 1968, and based on oneness, about learning one's ego process and the way to transcend that into Higher States of Mind to our "True Essential Self." This ritual acknowledges all the aspects of the deceased person's life as a way to send the Eternal Presence of Light to them wherever they are in their present stage of evolution since death. All the friends and family that attend send love, light and unity to the deceased loved one with the wish for their highest possible transcendence. The altar is set up and organized in a very prescribed way with candles and small bowls in each corner – filled with rice, water, oil or salt, each having a specific meaning. Ten people sign up to each lead a part of the ceremony process, each going up to the altar, reading the script, lighting a candle, following the steps and leading the chant that everyone says together. It was sacred and beautiful. I felt grounded and supported doing this ceremony with good friends and family. It was a lovely way of honoring Mike and sending him on his way.

Sunday, December 13th, the day of the memorial, we arrived for set up at 1:00 pm, bringing photos of Mike, candles, guest book pages and printed programs. Joan and Leslie arrived with the flowers. Karen and John set up the sound system, and the videographer was ready. Diana and Kay staffed the guest book which was half sheets of parchment paper for people to write a memory about Mike or a comment. I planned to put them all together in a book afterwards. Background guitar music started and guests began arriving thirty minutes before the service began.

Here's the Memorial Program handed out to all that attended:

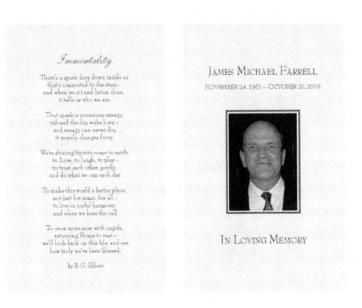

Immortality

There's a spark deep down inside us
that's connected to the stars -
and when we sit and listen close,
it tells us who we are.

That spark is conscious energy,
infused the day we're born -
and energy can never die,
it merely changes form.

We're shining Spirits come to earth,
to Love, to laugh, to play -
to treat each other gently,
and do what we can each day

To make this world a better place,
not just for some, for all -
to live in joyful harmony,
and when we hear the call

To once more soar with angels,
returning Home to rest -
we'll look back on this life, and see
how truly we've been blessed.

by B.G. Elbert

JAMES MICHAEL FARRELL

NOVEMBER 24, 1961 – OCTOBER 21, 2009

IN LOVING MEMORY

To start the service, Katherine welcomed everyone and invited all to sing the Loving Kindness chant led by Karen. Afterwards, Katherine said a prayer, introduced Mike's family members present, and told Mike's life story. It was then time for people to come up and speak. I was the first one. I walked to the microphone. I found my voice was a bit wobbly at first. Here's what I said,

"My darling husband Mike.

"It is a bummer that he took off his earth suit so soon. In some ways, I thought we were just getting started on our life together. I could see how we were both sanding off the bumps and corners of each other as we evolved our life together. I do know that in pushing the eject button on his earth suit, Mike realized a more expansive sense of who he is – that Love Life essence that never changes.

"Over the past few months prior to Mike's transition, I had been noticing and appreciating the ordinariness of our relationship – the everyday little things. Just having Mike at home – whether he was napping or reading or cooking together or watching a movie with Esther. We loved dinner and a movie at home or going out. We loved to cook and entertain our friends. It was fun to plan what we were each going to make. I do have to mention his amazing lobster bisque. One sip and I wanted to marry him. Thank goodness this is one recipe that IS written down.

"I would tell Mike how much I loved having him drive – even if when we were walking hand in hand – which is what we did when we were walking. Crossing the street, he would hold my hand back a bit, checking to make sure it was safe and then we'd continue. If I tripped, he'd grab my hand tighter and catch me. I could look around and not worry and be the passenger while walking!

"Mike was my anchor. I was his nest. We had a very strong, deep connection. Our connection was like a piece of cloth – you can't tell where one ends and the other begins. We had the ESP communication connection that I have had with a few close friends over the years, although never with a partner before Mike.

"I'm learning a new way to connect with Mike now. At our essence.

"I have this visual of a diving bell – the big suit worn for going into the depths of the sea – with a hose at the top connected to the air/oxygen – which is all around us. The diving bell is the body. Our life essence is inside the suit – it enlivens the suit – it is the sparkling Love Light energy that is everywhere. Within and without. I can consciously breathe in that essence and connect with Mike. Please, let's all take a deep breath together.

"I am blessed and so grateful to have had sweet darling Mike in my life for the gift of the time we shared. I am also grateful for the continuing love and connection with Mike's family.

"I thank you all for your love and for being here today."

Next up to speak was Wayne, Mike's good friend and best man. And then others came up and spoke including my brother, Hunter. Katherine introduced Karen to sing the song, "For Good." I wiped my eyes all the way through that.

Katherine spoke of the purpose for the day:

"At a time like this we have a human need to understand death. We are more than what we see, and more than what we cannot see. What we are seeking to understand, our soul already knows, even if we're not in touch with it. To consider Mike and the life that was lived and the work that was done, is to consider the energy of life as ongoing. I believe Life holds the bigger picture of our soul's journey, and I believe Life is everlasting. We were immortal before we took this body, and I believe Mike is experiencing the next era of immortality in his life, that death is just a doorway into the next expression…, the time after this earthly experience. I believe he is part of a continuity, and it is more expansive, and love is even stronger than it is here… Love moving into more love. Let us take a moment of silence, close our eyes if that's comfortable, and feel the love that is in our heart for Mike, and for other people that are dear to us who have made this transition… Let this passage be a reminder for us to savor our blessings, to speak from our heart and say the things that are important, and not leave anything unsaid. We never know when any of us will be called through this doorway."

We ended first with Mike's favorite chant, "I am Opening Up in Sweet Surrender," and finally with a closing prayer.

Chairs were removed, and the space became the reception. Wine and other beverages were served and hors d'oeuvres passed. So many of my friends said they wanted a service like this when they died. And, would I please plan and coordinate it?! Hard to know how to answer that. Looking back, I would say I was a bit numb by this point – what with all the planning and coordination plus the emotion of the moment. I'm very glad I had the program recorded as I really didn't catch everything that was said at the time.

I did so appreciate everyone that came that day. It is reassuring and supportive having friends and family close during a time like this. The reception lasted about two hours with much sharing and connecting. After the guests departed, we started collecting everything to take home. I ended up taking home the three large beautiful floral arrangements.

All the family members were invited to dinner at Hunter and Leslie's house. That included Mike's sisters and brother-in-law, my cousins, Kay and my daughter. When I read that on the event timeline, I thought how nice of them to do that. Do I remember being there? No. I do remember dinner the next night at a restaurant with

Moira, Cecelie, Pete, Kay and Esther before all departed the next day.

Look up the words to the song, "For Good" from the Broadway show, *Wicked*, by composer Stephen Schwartz.

https://www.stephenschwartz.com/works/wicked/

Memorial Week Timeline

Tuesday, December 8

3:15 PM   Kay arrives OAK SW #1988. Marinda picks up.

Thursday, December 10

4:00 PM   Marinda & Kay take Mini to Casa Madrona Hotel – 801 Bridgeway, Sausalito.

9:14 PM   Pete & Cec arrive OAK Alaska Air #354 (Seattle). Marinda & Kay pick up – take to Casa Madrona.

Friday, December 11

3:39 PM   Moira arrives SFO UA 305 Terminal 3. Hunter to pick up and take to Casa Madrona Hotel – 801 Bridgeway, Sausalito.

4:00 PM   Marinda – Meditation class

5:00 PM   Whitney arrives SFO – Morgan to pick her up – go to Hunter & Leslie's home.

6:00 PM-   Dinner at Hunter & Leslie's – Whitney,
ish   Morgan, Esther, Kay

Saturday, December 12

12:00 PM   Lunch at Marinda's – Kay, Esther, Moira, Cec, Pete, Morgan, Whitney, Diana (Marinda to give maps/directions for Black Earth, Servino's & H&L's)

3:30 PM	Marinda & Kay go to Novato home for client event set up (drop off chocolate, wine, clothing for pm)
7:15-7:20 PM	Arrive for Black Earth Ceremony – Marinda & Kay; Moira, Cec & Pete; Morgan, Whitney, Esther & Diana (3 cars)
7:30 PM	Black Earth Ceremony. 9:00 PM reception – wine & chocolates.

Sunday, December 13

12:00 PM	Room set at Servino Ristorante (9 Main Street, Tiburon)
1:00 PM	Joan & Leslie arrive at Servino's with flowers
	Karen Drucker & John Hoy arrive – set up in front left corner by doors to deck
	Marinda, Esther, Kay arrives. Bring photos, candle, cloth, programs. Set up guest book.
	Rev. Katherine Revoir
1:30 PM	John Van Daam, California Video arrives
	Programs handed out by Deborah Erwin, guest book – Kay & Diana
	Background music playing – John.
	Guests begin to arrive.
2:00 PM	Service begins – Rev. Katherine Revoir
3:00 PM	Service over, Reception begins – food and beverages.
5:00 PM	Reception over, guests depart.

Saturday, December 12

6:00 PM   Soups on at Hunter & Leslie's – gathering for
            Marinda, Esther, Kay, Moira, Pete, Cec,
            Morgan, Whitney

Monday, December 14

8:30 AM   Whitney departs SFO – Morgan to take her

6:00 PM   Dinner gathering – Marinda, Esther, Moira,
            Cec, Pete (The Spinnaker restaurant)

Tuesday, December 15

1:09 PM   Moira departs SFO UA 5860 Terminal One.
            10:00 am – drive her to airport.

12:28 PM   Cec & Pete depart OAK USO 2641 – 10:30 am
            drive them to airport

Wednesday, December 16

1:30 PM   Kay departs OAK SW #577. Marinda to take
            her at 11:30 am.

My Story

I started questioning what is death? . . . ever since my mother died when I was ten. I wanted to know what is death? Does healing occur at this transition? What happens?

My mother died in the Spring when I was ten years old. She had been ill and had moved six months prior to my grandmother's house with a Christian Science nurse attending her. At that age, it felt like she had been gone a year from our home. We did go visit her at my grandmother's house. It was quite a shocking surprise when I was told my mother had died. She was an artist, an amazing cook and seamstress. She decorated our home, sewed the curtains, made many of our clothes and hers and sewed items for an annual holiday bazaar. I have photos of us modeling mother daughter aprons, and my father and brother modeling matching work aprons. I have the pattern she created and used to make tea cozies. She showed me how to color with my crayons in a circular motion to create depth. I remember posing for paintings she did of me. She painted a scene on one wall in the kitchen of an open window, shutters opening out to the view of the town down below and a spit of land reaching out into the ocean. It was not unusual for guests to bump their head on the wall trying to look out the window.

My mother was tall – 5'8", slim with dark hair. She was always beautifully dressed and entertained with style. Although I didn't recognize that her entertaining – cooking delicious food and setting beautiful tables – was a "style" until much later in my life. When you grow up with something, you don't realize it's something special until you can compare it. Perhaps, because her mother ran a Swedish Tea Room in Chicago when she was growing up, that had influenced my mother's sense of style and entertaining.

We lived on a dead-end street. Every summer there was a block party and my mother always helped with the decorations. The kids had games and activities during the day and the parents danced in the evening. And she was an amazing photo stylist – although I didn't know that term back then. Every year, my father would take a Christmas picture – the first few years were just me starting at three months old propped between bookends wearing a halo and wings. My mother created the halo and wings, the lettering that said, "Merry Christmas," or whatever the decor was that she created for that year's photo. When I was three, I was holding my brother up to stand. At five, I was cradling my baby sister, and she, my brother and I were dressed in flannel choir robes she had made. My father would take the pictures, print them and mail them off to their friends.

I learned to cook by my mother's side, starting with Toll House chocolate chip cookies. I made her a birthday cake when I was five with my children's baking set. At age eight, she and Aunt Alice, my father's sister, went to New York City for two weeks. My mother gave me two children's cookbooks, and I cooked dinner every night for two weeks. I loved it. Tuna chip casserole anyone?

There was talk about hiring a housekeeper after my mother died so we could stay in the house, but my father was not able to handle that. So, he sold the house, and we all moved into my grandmother's, his mother's, house. My younger brother, sister and I were sent off to a Christian Science boarding school for four years and lived with our father and grandmother when not in school. The boarding school was the same one that my mother raised money for with the things she made for their annual holiday bazaar. I was raised in Christian Science, attending Sunday School from the time I was a young child. My grandmother had been raised a Quaker. When she married my grandfather and moved from Indiana to the suburbs of Chicago, she found the local Christian Science church to be the closest to her Quaker faith and she raised her three children in Christian Science.

Every morning at boarding school, there was quiet time to read the weekly lesson. This practice of reading spiritual ideas and principles and studying statements of truth to gain understanding became a foundation for my life. I understood that I had the power to affect my world, my situations, and if I found myself in a place that was challenging in some way, the answer was not out there. It was an inside job. In boarding school, I learned to solve physical and school problems by cracking open my books and studying the true reality of the situation and demonstrating my understanding with a healing of the situation or physical problem.

During my high school freshman year away at boarding school, I discovered a way to think differently about my mother's death. Being at a Christian Science school, we attended Sunday School and Wednesday evening services where anyone had the opportunity to stand up and share their experiences and healings. One Wednesday evening, a young man stood up and told about a death in his family and how it was like they were walking along a path together and a brick wall came up between them. They were still walking together but could no longer see each other. That helped me a lot in seeing death as a doorway where connection remains even though they are gone from our presence physically.

When I was fourteen, my father bought a house again, near where we had lived before my mother died, and I started my sophomore year of high school with students I knew from elementary school. As the oldest, my responsibilities at home were cooking dinner every night and keeping an eye on my brother and especially my sister, who was developmentally disabled. Back then they called it mildly retarded. I loved to cook, and I loved fashion. I made all my own clothes in high school, perusing fashion magazines and finding patterns that I could adapt to what I found in the magazines.

When I got to college in Indiana, I studied and learned more about other religions. From college, I moved to school in New York and began my career in fashion at Macy's Herald Square. I then moved to San Francisco. My uncle introduced me to books – *Seth Speaks* and *The Nature of Personal Reality* by Jane Roberts and *The Kin of Ata are Waiting for You* by Dorothy Bryant – giving me a more expanded view of what is the true reality of our experience here on this plane of existence. I was also exploring what is healing? How does it occur? Was my mother healed when she made her transition out of the body? I used my body as my own healing laboratory. I spent a year working in Tokyo which also opened my eyes to other ways of viewing life. There is such a sense of beauty and esthetics that the Japanese have. Learning the language also helped me understand the culture.

Throughout my career, whether living in New York, Connecticut or San Francisco, I continued to read and study. I always had a book on my bedside table. I studied meditation with a teacher, who also taught *A Course in Miracles*. Reading many books, I discovered many ways of saying the same thing using different language and ideas. With different words – facets of the same truths, I grew to have a greater understanding of spiritual principles from various philosophies.

I moved back to the San Francisco Bay Area with my husband just before my daughter was born. When my daughter was three, I got divorced and became a single mom. I was determined to spend my time focusing on my daughter and my work and did not date at all. I joined the Religious Science church in town as a focus for spiritual community for myself and my daughter. I got involved with the youth church and took classes for four years to become a Religious Science Practitioner, a teacher and spiritual counselor. During the four years of study, we read books about death – the classic, *On Death and Dying* by Elizabeth Kubler-Ross and Stephen Levine's books, *A Year to Live: How to Live this Year as If It Were Your Last* and *Who Dies?: An Investigation of Conscious Living and Conscious Dying*. My spiritual practice and study over so many years gave me a foundation, a grounding that supported me when I found out that Mike had died so suddenly.

I had heard many stories about women reconnecting with men they had known in college or in the past. This was in 1999. I asked the Universe, "Who would that be for me?" A few months later I received a letter in the mail from the man I dated in college. He lives in Florida, was divorced and had one daughter in her twenties. My daughter was eight at this time. We met in Southern CA one weekend when he was there for business. It was great to catch up, however, I wasn't interested in a long-distance relationship. After about six months, I asked the Universe, "What about someone that lives closer to me?" A couple of months later, May 1st, 2000, I received a call from the man I almost married in June 1972. I had sent out wedding invitations and then sent out cancellation notices. A very good decision on my part. He was living in the East Bay. The first thing he did was apologize for his past behavior (I won't get into that story!) and asked if we could get together. I was so shocked to hear from him after all this time that I said yes. I don't even know how he got my number. Maybe from the Universal Operator? We dated for about eight months. Again, I realized that this was not the man I wanted to spend my life with. So, we parted ways, and I never heard from him again. I decided I was NOT going to ask the Universe again, who was the man for me, and I put my head down and went to work – working on myself. I know it's always an inside job. Whatever is happening "out there" is a reflection of what's going on inside. I focused on doing my personal growth work, my event business and my daughter.

It took my dear friends, Gayle and Wayne, to introduce the right man for me. He ended up in my house. I didn't have to go anywhere to find him!

Chapter Two
At the Station

After the four events and the two memorials (yes, they were events, too), I was finally ready to start the blog I agreed with Mike to write.

Flowers

January 21, 2010
I've always wondered why flowers are sent to the family of the deceased. Now I have a different understanding of why this is a tradition and a way to express condolences.

Flowers are alive, fresh. A reminder of life. Flowers also have powerful emotional and spiritual healing properties. The floral arrangements I received were a reminder of the love and support of those that sent them to me – every time I looked at them and appreciated their beauty.

Going Deeper

January 27, 2010

Reading about grief in *Emotional Genius*, by Karla McLaren affirms what my spiritual and intellectual quadrants know without a doubt – that Mike knows himself to be expansive Love and Light – and consciousness. Who he is has not changed, except he has taken off his earth suit.

And . . . I must dive deep into my body and emotional quadrants. To cry the tears that release the stuckness of shock. To dive into the depths of the sorrow – to the sacred connections with our ancestors, loved ones and all of Life. To "connect to the healing energies inside grief" – and immerse myself in the waters of my emotions. The body knows about grief and what to do. I am listening.

Erasing the Blackboard

February 20, 2010

All the plans – such as gatherings with friends, the dreams
– retiring to Hawaii, the trips we were planning – to visit
Mike's sister and husband in the UK and at their house in
France, to visit New York City which Mike had never been
to – even though he'd lived or traveled to over forty-nine
countries. All these and many more desires that we had
talked about . . . I now am erasing from the blackboard.
Those plans don't apply now. Well, some do – I will still
go visit friends in New York and visit his sister and her
husband in the UK and France – just not with Mike. We
talked about going to Esalen Institute in Big Sur – he had
been and said it was so wonderful. Maybe I will go . . .
and, it will be different without him.

In the book, *Spiritual Liberation*, by Michael
Beckwith, he says: "Surrender is a bold spiritual stance, the
stance of a spiritual warrior, because what we are
surrendering to is the next stage of our evolution." I am
surrendering to a new next stage of my evolution, wiping
the blackboard clean to start again.

Appreciating the Ordinary

March 3, 2010

It is a bummer that Mike took off his earth suit so soon. In some ways, I thought we were just getting started on our life together. We'd been married for just four-and-a-half years. I could see how we were both sanding off the bumps and corners of each other as we evolved our life together. I do know that in pushing the eject button on his earth suit, Mike realized a more expansive sense of who he is – that Love Life essence that never changes.

Over the past few months prior to Mike's transition, I had been noticing and appreciating the ordinariness of our relationship – the everyday little things. Just having Mike at home – whether he was napping or reading, or cooking together, or watching a movie together with our daughter. We loved dinner and a movie at home or going out. We loved to cook and entertain our friends. It was fun to plan what we were each going to make. I do have to mention his amazing lobster bisque. One sip and I wanted to marry him. I am grateful that I was noticing and appreciating the ordinary gems in our relationship. I miss both of us cooking in the kitchen together – it is what our remodeled kitchen was designed for. I miss the we.

Connecting Through the Veil

March 12, 2010

I had a few very clear instances of Mike's presence – of reaching through the veil to me. Within the first few days after his death, there was a message on my cell phone – a whispered, "I love you." It had to be Mike. I've read about these occurrences.

They fill the top of the dresser in our master bedroom with family photos and other special objects. Next to Mike's photo, I placed the small flat metal heart I had given him right after we were married – and that he carried every day in his pocket with his change. On one side is engraved, Love Flows Through Me, and on the other side, Love Surrounds Me. When I looked the next day, I discovered the heart had moved. Guess who?

A few weeks after Mike's death, I went upstairs to the bedroom and found the room filled with the strong smell of coffee. There was no coffee being made downstairs in the kitchen. I knew it was Mike. He had coffee every morning.

I recommend reading the book, *Hello from Heaven*, by Bill & Judy Guggenheim. It helped validate for me the after-death communications I had from Mike were not unusual.

In the Goo

April 2, 2010

When I was first reeling from the news of Mike's death, the image that came to mind was of turning into goo – just like a caterpillar does. It deconstructs in the cocoon and melts into goo. The imaginal cells then move into action to reform the goo into a butterfly. I was pushed into the goo. I feel like I am still in the goo now. Sometimes I feel like I have an inkling of what's next, that my imagination, my imaginal cells, are creating something new. It's not yet clear, it's still mostly goo.

A few weeks later, a second image came to mind . . . I was flattened like Bozo the Clown. When I was a child, we had a blow-up punching bag of Bozo the Clown. You could punch it to the ground, and it would right itself because of the weighted bottom. I feel like I was punched to the ground. There are times when it seems I am righting myself, and other times when I am flattened again. Bozo always came back to standing up and I know I will, too.

Emptying the Closet and Deleting Emails

April 7, 2010

This last week has been transforming, cathartic, sad, grieving, digging up soil that hadn't been turned yet . . . turning up items of Mike's that I'd stuffed in drawers – till later. I had shelves and rods installed in the master closet a week ago. Which meant I had to empty the closet. This also meant that I had to go through everything in the closet. No more waiting. As I put things away, I cried, wishing Mike were here. I'm washing lots of clothes as I sort through it all – what to keep, what to pass on. Cleaning. Clearing. Working in my closet. Seems like inner work to me. Feels like it, too. Lots of grieving. Changing the inside as I change the outside.

After a week plus of closet work, I found myself drawn to clean out my email in and out boxes. My inbox messages had been filed a couple months ago, but I had not cleared the outbox since before Mike passed on. I found emails I had sent to him and a few from him – more dipping into the depths of what was. . . that is no longer. I cried and pushed the delete button on the emails. There's no deleting him from my heart.

The Firsts Keep Coming

May 19, 2010

It seems like the first year is the most difficult. There have so many firsts without Mike. Halloween. Thanksgiving. His Birthday – that day felt really empty. Christmas. New Year's. Valentine's Day. I thought about him a lot. He made a big deal of Valentine's Day. He surprised me each year with a special gift and card. I'd never had a man be so thoughtful and loving with this holiday. Easter. Our wedding anniversary – I wrote April 6th for two days in a row until I realized why. I had forgotten our anniversary a couple times before. I was always happy he remembered it. Much harder was April 21st – six months since Mike departed this life experience. Every time I thought of this, tears sprung to my eyes. It seemed like it had been so recently and yet, so long ago. I couldn't really write about it till now.

This timeframe feels like a milestone in accepting the reality that Mike's not here. I keep reflecting on Joan Didion's book, *The Year of Magical Thinking*. It took a year for her to really accept – or begin to accept – that her husband was gone. More holidays and remembrances to come. Memorial Day. Fourth of July – last year we were at Dillon Beach, as usual. My girlfriend, Kim, and I have been going with our daughters every year for ten years. It was so wonderful to have Mike there, too. We all had so much fun. I know I will miss him being there this year.

At first, it felt uncomfortable driving Mike's Mini Cooper. It smells like Mike, my daughter said. It did. I felt like I was surrounded by him. He loved his Mini. Years ago, I read that items that are well loved hold that love energy and you can feel that attraction, that love. I have experienced this with rings – my mother's, my grandmothers', and Mike's mother's – and with the Mini. I'm driving it more now. The scent is beginning to fade, or perhaps, I'm getting more used to it.

Saying Goodbye Again

May 20, 2010

Swirling ashes and flowers at the ocean's edge

Last weekend, I flew to Hawaii for a few days to join friends for a classic Hawaiian weaving workshop at Kona Village. I wove bracelets. I was also there to release Mike's ashes into the ocean. He always wanted to retire to Hawaii. We decided to gather Sunday morning – about sixteen of us. I am so grateful for all that came together as I needed everyone's help to make this ceremony happen.

I had never opened the shopping bag holding the box of ashes after I picked it up in Orange County. It sat in the closet till I packed the shopping bag with the box in my suitcase for the flight to the Big island. Only just before the ceremony did I take the box out of the bag . . . and discovered that the box was a heavy metal box – sealed shut, with no way to open it. I had asked for a plain box. Who knew? Two men in our group both tried to open it and called it a safe, not a box. The handyman at Kona Village Resort was called to bring his tools. As he was figuring out how to open the box, he asked, "Did he really like this place?" Yes, actually he did. Success – the box was finally pried open.

The ceremony began a little later than originally planned and it was perfect. Including trying to get Mike out of the box. One suggested a tide pool at the ocean's edge was a good place on this balmy, windy day. Another provided a basket to put the bag of ashes in. A special friend wore a sarong in Mike's honor, as Mike would have worn one if he had been here. Another was wearing a look-alike to Mike's favorite sarong. She had bought it at the market just a few days before – colors she didn't usually wear but it had called to her! Aloha, Mike.

We all filed down to the tide pool and gathered in a half circle. I said a few words about Mike – about the joy and love that connected us to Mike and to each other. I hadn't been to this resort since our honeymoon. Now Mike and I were both here again. We prayed and sang the chant – "There is only one of us, in your eyes it's me I see, there is only one of us, you are my reflection, there is only one." I stood barefoot in the water and with "Amazing Grace" being played on the harmonica, I poured Mike's ashes slowly into the water as the waves rolled in and out. The fine silver-grey powder mixed and swirled with the water – stirring and flowing into a larger and larger area at the edge of the ocean. We broke our leis and tossed the flowers into the water – a mix of peach, pink, purple and white floating above the moving misty water. The mist didn't go out to sea as much as dissolve and merge with the water and drift down into the sand at the water's edge. I guess he's not leaving the beach. We gathered back on the sand and many expressed how beautiful the ceremony was. One said that this is how he wants to go – so simple and so moving.

When I was pouring the fine ashes into the water, I flashed on how this is what Andy Goldsworthy does . . . grinding up natural elements and pouring the colored powder down a river or stream. Here I was making art – the ephemeral art of life – watching and remembering sweet Mike.

Cooking with Mike

July 12, 2010
I miss cooking with Mike. Our large, remodeled kitchen was perfect for two chefs – two sinks, two areas for prep and lots of counter space. Going through papers, I found a menu for a dinner party we had hosted on October 11, 2008 for family and friends:

An Indian Summer Dinner for Six

Halibut baked in Parchment with Garlic and Rosemary
Eggplant, Tomato, Onion Gratin
Fresh Corn and Fava Bean Salad with Roasted Garlic Vinaigrette
New Potatoes with Parsley and Butter
Mixed Greens with Apple, Orange, Avocado and a Citrus Vinaigrette
Fresh Peach Tart
Homemade Chocolate Almond Truffles

The halibut was Mike's recipe – delicious and easy. I don't think I've made it since he's been gone. I bought fava beans and corn on the cob last week at the Farmers' Markets to make the salad for the first time since last summer. It was a favorite recipe of ours.

Ours. I miss that – sharing things that were our favorites . . . our "dinner and a movie" nights, our gatherings with friends, reading the Sunday papers together. Last year at this time, Mike was helping me pit apricots for jam. I've been stirring all evening and have made four batches of apricot jam. Next week I'll get another case from the farmers' market and make apricot butter, which is my favorite. Both are enjoyed by all that receive them at Christmas.

Blog Response to Cooking with Mike

July 12, 2010

    KayC

I love this picture and this story. I resisted opening the notification announcing this new post...I resisted what I thought was going to make me sad. But it didn't make me sad. It brought Mike and the apricots right here to my monitor and the healing is apparent. He made me smile, and so did your rich memories. And I think I wore that shirt as I worked in the garden today. Harvest time and tomato pie is next. Mike would love tomato pie.

    Hugs and love to you...your precious gifts are received and appreciated.

Halibut Baked in Parchment

    4 pieces of halibut (1 per person)
    Fresh garlic, sliced
    EV Olive oil
    Rosemary
    Parchment paper
    Set oven to 400 degrees.

Tear off four good-size pieces of parchment paper. Brush olive oil in a spot in the middle of the parchment. Place the halibut on top of the brushed-on olive oil. Place sliced pieces of garlic on top of the halibut. Add a sprig of rosemary on top of the fish. Fold up the parchment, bringing two sides together and folding over the two sides together, then tuck the ends of the parchment under the fish, making a package. Place each parchment package on a cookie sheet and place in the oven for about 20 to 25 minutes. It's ok to open the parchment and check one of the fish to confirm it is cooked.

To serve, open the package using scissors. With a spatula, lift the fish up and place on each plate. Easy!

Fava Bean and Corn Salad with Roasted Garlic Vinaigrette

For the Salad:

2 cups shucked fava beans (3 lbs. fresh fava beans)

4 – 5 cups fresh corn kernels, cooked and cut off cobs (about 5 to 6 ears)

1 medium cucumber, quartered lengthwise and thinly sliced

1/2 red onion, chopped

2-3 Tablespoons chopped flat leaf parsley

3-4 ozs. Feta cheese

1. Prepare the fava beans. Shuck the beans and blanch in boiling water for 3 to 5 minutes. Rinse under cold water or transfer to a bowl of water with ice to cool beans. Peel off outer clear coats on beans and set aside.

Cook corn for 10 minutes in boiling water. Remove and place on plate, cover with linen towel and let corn cool. Cut corn off cobs and put in a bowl for salad. Add fava beans, chopped onion, cucumber, parsley and crumbled feta and toss with vinaigrette.

For the vinaigrette:

1 head garlic

1 Tbsp extra virgin olive oil

3 tablespoons red wine vinegar

¾ teaspoon salt

¼ teaspoon red pepper flakes

Freshly ground pepper

1. Cut off top of garlic to reveal cloves. Drizzle with 1 teaspoon olive oil. Wrap in foil and bake at 350 degrees

for 1 hour. Cool and squeeze garlic from skins. Mash garlic cloves into a smooth paste.

2. Whisk remaining ingredients with roasted garlic.
3. Toss salad with vinaigrette.

Leslie's Mandarin Orange Salad

This is my sister-in-law, Leslie's, fabulous salad. It's so good and easy – and fresh tasting. Yes, it was part of that dinner party menu.

Salad:
Mixed greens
1 can mandarin oranges, drained (or remove rind and pith from an orange and cut into slices or segments)
3 – 4 sliced green onions
1 avocado, cubed
1 crisp apple, chopped
Toasted sliced almonds

Dressing:
1/4 cup sugar
1/4 cup red wine vinegar
1/2 cup olive oil salt, pepper...couple dashes of Tabasco.
Shake together. Put in 'fridge for 15 minutes.

Clean the mixed greens.
Prep the orange and green onions – put in separate containers.
Cut the apple and avocado at the last moment before mixing the salad together and tossing with the dressing. Sprinkle the toasted almonds on top of the salad.
Enjoy!

Apricot Jam

10 cups halved apricots
5 cups sugar
1/4 cup lemon juice
1 Tbsp coconut oil or butter

Put apricots in a pot with sugar, lemon juice and 1/4 cup water over very low heat. Once sugar starts to melt, stir until dissolved. Bring to a boil then reduce to a simmer. At this point, add 1 Tbsp coconut oil or butter. The fat eliminates the foam. Simmer apricots, stirring often – more so as it gets thicker.

Have a couple saucers in the freezer. To check if jam is ready to can, put a dab of jam on the plate and put it back in the freezer to cool. If there is no liquid around the jam, it is ready to can.

Ladle into clean jars and seal. Process in a hot water bath for 10 minutes for pints or 1/2 pints.

Rings and Things

August 28, 2010

I've been pondering the question of whether I should continue to wear my wedding band, or . . . why do I continue to wear my wedding band? When I got divorced from my first husband, I willingly took off my ring. It's not like that this time. When Mike and I arranged our wedding in a week, he insisted on getting wedding bands for both of us. I thought it would take too long to get them ordered, etc. We both found rings at the first store we shopped. Mike's band fit perfectly. I had mine resized after the ceremony. Is there a time limit on how long to wear my ring? It goes so perfectly with the solitaire that was his mum's.

It's weird. I wear my wedding rings and think of Mike. I see Mike all around me – his furniture in every room. In some rooms it's all his furniture. Our furniture melded together when we merged our lives. So did our kitchen pots and pans, knives and dishes. A good friend said to Mike, "Didn't you know you were meant to be together, since your furniture goes so well together?" Now I am left with the furniture – and no Mike. Don't get me wrong; I love the furniture and everything in the kitchen. I just wish I had Mike instead. (Here's that magical thinking Joan Didion wrote about.) It feels like I have the leftovers, no matter how wonderful those things are.

Speaking of Joan Didion, I read her book, *The Year of Magical Thinking*, two years ago and last year, I read Christopher Buckley's *Losing Mum and Pup*. Reading these books turned out to be preparation for where I am now. Both books have provided me with references and ways to think about my experience of loss – and the process – of time and thoughts and questions that arise.

When I write these posts, I mull over the ideas and the words to use. Weeks have gone by thinking, writing, adding, deleting, rewriting. For now, I'm letting go of the question about wearing my rings. I'm done focusing on this – time to move on. The answer will be revealed in its right way and right time. When I take my wedding rings off, there's an indentation that remains on my finger... just like Mike has left an impression on my heart that will always be there.

Blog Response to Rings and Things

October 18, 2010

Hi Marinda.

Today I received your card and introduction to your blog, which I have really enjoyed reading... thanks!

Why do you continue to wear your wedding ring? Why do I continue to keep Mike's name and contact info on my cell phone? My wife asks me the same thing. It's simple, when I scroll through looking for names, I invariably see Mike's name and when I do I think about him and, if only briefly, they are fond thoughts. My answer? I like seeing Mike Farrell appear when scrolling for other friends and I like that it reminds me of him.

Take care, Ian.

After Saying Goodbye

September 2010

I finally got a card off to friends to let them know about the ceremony in Hawaii, scattering his ashes in the ocean at Kona Village. And, I let them know about my blog.

On Sunday, May 16th friends gathered on the Big Island of Hawaii
for a simple and beautiful ceremony.
We gathered in a half circle at the beach around a tidepool.
We prayed, said a few words about Mike - about the joy and love
that connected us to Mike and to each other,
and with Amazing Grace playing on a harmonica ...
I poured Mike's ashes slowly into the water as the waves rolled in and out.
The fine silver grey powder mixed and swirled with the water -
stirring and flowing into a larger and larger area at the edge of the ocean.
We broke our leis and tossed the flowers into the water -
a mix of peach, pink, purple and white floating above the moving misty water.
The mist didn't go out to sea as much as dissolve and merge with the water
and drift down into the sand at the waters edge.
He's not leaving the beach.
This is where Mike always wanted to retire.

November 24, 1951-
October 21, 2009

In **January**, I started a *blog* about
my thoughts and feelings of being a widow.

There's more about the ceremony in Hawaii, about flowers and other memories and experiences
at http://widowzhealing.wordpress.com/
I invite you to make a comment on the blog, sign up for my intermittant posts,
or forward to someone you know who might benefit from reading it.

I want you to know how much I appreciated your cards, phone calls, emails, and beautiful flowers -
reminding me of the love and support that you sent with them.

Thank you for being in my life and in Mike's life.

With much gratitude, love and blessings,

Marinda
September 2010

Chapter Three
Departing and Arriving

A New Year

January 3, 2011

It's been quite a while since I added a post. In mid-September, I attended my annual WomanSpirit retreat – five wonderful days among the redwoods with girlfriends and one hundred other women. Last year, Mike helped us load up the car and then he stayed home and relaxed. This year, I took Mike with me – bringing his drum to play and thinking about him a lot. My friend, Sara, who is a medium, was there and told me that Mike was standing right next to me, so I guess he did tag along. I thought I would write about this after our retreat, but I wasn't ready to do so.

October 21st was the anniversary of Mike making his sudden transition – exiting his earth suit. I scheduled a phone session with Sara to check in with Mike after one year of him being gone. I'm not sure what I expected to learn, but I just really felt I needed to check in with Mike. He was right there by Sara and available for the reading. Sara said he had been eagerly waiting for the session to begin. What did I learn? Mike's good and I'm still adjusting to this change and the love is there, strong and clear, no matter what.

I didn't realize what a hard day that would be and was grateful I had a dinner scheduled with friends that evening. I brought one of Mike's bottles of red wine to share and we toasted him. I thought I would write something that day, however; I discovered there was still much to be processed before I could write again. At this point, a year had passed – beyond the "remembering what Mike was doing last year at this time." So much for it being easier, it just seems more final. I think a part of me has been in shock all year. Now the reality and more grieving are present.

November 24th was Mike's birthday. Last year, I had bought a Kindle a few months before his birthday and was looking forward to giving it to him as he loved to read. The Kindle sat in the drawer for a year. I didn't know who to give it to. In November, I had to file some papers with the county clerk. The gal behind the counter was telling me about a drawing they were having in the office and the prize was a Kindle. She really wanted it – she loved to read. It seemed like the signal to me, and a week later I went back to see her and gave her the Kindle. It surprised me that I cried afterwards.

December 25th – We celebrated Christmas out of town this year. I didn't want to repeat our usual traditions at home that had included Mike. We would gather in the living room and open the gifts in our Christmas stockings. We would then take a break and have brunch with smoked salmon, bagels, cream cheese, capers, red onion and squeezed lemon – and champagne. There was sparkling cider for my daughter. And then we would return to open the rest of the gifts. Each of us taking a turn to open one. For a change, my daughter and I went to Santa Fe for the week of Christmas. It was very relaxing, with help from some massages at the hotel spa. I rarely stop and rest – something Mike was great at. We visited with family and friends, walked around the square, checked out shops and museums, and enjoyed local restaurants. Christmas Eve we joined friends for the Luminaria Walk down Canyon

Road – classic Santa Fe. I thought I would write this blog while I was there – but no; it was time to just stop. Mike would have been proud of me.

I've spent some time going through photos of the past few years. Mike didn't like to get his photo taken, but I managed to have some taken. I even had photos taken that I thought I would send as a Christmas or New Year's card. That never happened, although now I can show a photo with no complaints from Mike, just lots of memories.

Leaving on a Jet Plane

April 15, 2011

So much time has passed, and changes are occurring. I took off my wedding band a few weeks ago. I decided I didn't need to wear it any longer. I'm not married anymore – except in my heart. I continue to wear the diamond ring Mike gave me – it's got all the love energy in it. The ring was his mum's. She bought it with lottery winnings. She had always wanted a large diamond solitaire. She told Mike it would be his later on. Mike's mum died when he was 16 years old. When Mike father died about ten years later, he got the ring. And then he carried it around the world for the next twenty-five years – working in places like South America, Thailand, Saudi Arabia and northern Canada. He never married during all this time. His work managing multi-billion-dollar construction projects didn't allow much time for relationships. There is a lot of love in this ring and I feel it.

I'm off for a vacation to Bali with five girlfriends. Mike and I had talked about him doing one more construction project at a location around the world. The one he wanted to help manage was in Australia – just a short plane ride away from Bali. I keep thinking about this and our plans for this project as I pack to go. I still miss him a lot.

After Bali

July 7, 2011

I took one of Mike's sarongs with me on my trip to Bali. He had lived in Thailand for two years and had collected some sarongs. My girlfriends and I stayed two nights at a resort on the ocean near the island of Manganyan, known for some of the best snorkeling in the world – amazing fish in wild colors and beautiful coral. We spent a day on the water riding out to the island and snorkeling in two different areas. We got soaked in a rainstorm mid-day. Back at the resort, I hung my sarong up to dry . . . and left it behind by mistake when we left the next morning. Although it turned out it really wasn't a mistake. In fact, I had a bit of premonition that it might happen when I packed the sarong. I obviously needed to leave a bit of Mike in Bali. It felt right. Mike and I had talked about living there part time while he worked on a project in Australia. It was to be his last time working at a project site.

I've been back from Bali for two months. It seems shorter than that. I went with the intention to give myself the gift of a break from all that has occurred the past two-plus years. Unplugging and going to the flip side of the world is a real break from the day-to-day. And such a beautiful place to do it – with an incredibly wonderful group of girlfriends.

Since coming back from Bali, I discovered that I have been in a fog since Mike left this earth scene. A friend said it is a healing fog – cushioning the shock. It's been a year and eight months. The fog is lifting, and I am grieving again. Since all emotions are good, this must be the next step in accepting the change that has occurred with Mike being gone. I find myself weepy at odd times. I know to just let it out. I don't spend time figuring out why. More diving to the depths to release the grief and allow greater healing to occur. What I learned in Bali with my girlfriends when one would start getting teary . . . blubbering is good.

Second Anniversary

October 21, 2011

It felt necessary to have a ceremony for the Second Anniversary of Mike's death. I know that a ceremony can anchor time and place. For this occasion, it allows me to bring forward my memories of Mike, to honor him and acknowledge that two years had now passed. It seemed like yesterday and a long time ago at the same time. Why a ceremony for the second anniversary? When the first anniversary arrived, I could close the door on remembering what we had been doing together the year before at each time during that first year. With the second anniversary, there was more finality – at least that is how it seemed to me. No more harking back to what we had been doing. I had now filled in the space of two years without him.

My friend and minister, Katherine, suggested we create an altar and put things that Mike liked on it. Just the act of creating the altar was a ceremony giving me time to honor and think about Mike. I used the coffee table in the living room – and I "set the table" for Mike with things he valued and that I valued about him. I placed his favorite sarong with shades of teal and red on the table with the red beads he always wore with it when we sat in our meditation circle. Mike had lived in Thailand for two years and found sarongs more comfortable than jeans. When we would attend a day-long meditation retreat together, something we did two to three times a year, he would change from his jeans to a sarong. I still go – it is so grounding and centering – and I miss Mike sitting in the circle.

I collected photos – of our wedding day, a picture of Mike happy in Hawaii, one with two of his sisters, Moira and Cecelie, and a copy of his memorial program. I framed his Hawaii photo with large dark pink hydrangea from the garden. I opened a bottle of Mike's red wine (he didn't get to drink all those bottles he had collected and saved) and set out three glasses – for Katherine, Mike and me. Mike loved wine and cheese, so I served goat cheese with my homemade apricot chutney, crackers and fresh figs. I poured the wine into Mike's beautiful crystal decanter and then into our glasses. I lit the votive candles. Now we were ready to start the ceremony.

We stood in front of the altar and toasted Mike with his delicious red wine. Katherine read some quotes – here are two them I really appreciated. I think of them as prayers.

There's a Buddhist Sutra, or sacred text that says:

"Everything that has the nature to arise has the nature to pass away.
The person who knows this in their heart knows true happiness."

This quote by Paramahansa Yogananda is one of my favorites:

"The body is only a garment.
How many times have you changed your clothing in this life?
Yet because of this you would not say that YOU have changed.
Similarly, when you give up this bodily dress at death you do not change.
You are just the same, an immortal soul, a child of God."

We both shared remembrances of Mike. I spoke of happy times I had with Mike, entertaining our friends over dinners, cooking in the kitchen together, chilling out on the back deck in the summer with Mike's constant companion, our black cat, Thunder. Thunder would hang out wherever Mike was and follow him around. Mike had so many stories having lived all over the world for thirty years managing multi-billion-dollar construction projects. Besides Thailand, he lived in Venezuela, Scotland, Saudi Arabia to name just a few. I was amazed by the stories he told about surviving a helicopter crash into the Gulf of Mexico, a train accident, a sinking boat, and a plane accident. I figured he was a good bet to stay around a while if he had survived all that.

Katherine remembered the time she joined us to watch a movie on the big screen in our living room. She noticed how connected we were with each other. Katherine said she had never seen me in such an aligned and comfortable relationship, and she had known me for many years.

We both enjoyed the cheese and chutney on crackers and the figs with our delicious wine. I knew Mike would appreciate the offerings . . . and the stories.

Second Anniversary Recipe
Apricot Chutney

This is the recipe for the apricot chutney that I "served" on Mike's altar with goat cheese and crackers.

10 cups ripe apricots, halved and pitted
1 cup golden raisins
1 onion, finely chopped
2-3 garlic cloves, finely chopped
1 teaspoon coriander seeds
1-1/2 teaspoons grated or finely chopped fresh ginger
1 Tablespoon sea salt
1-1/2 cups light brown sugar
1-1/4 cups white wine vinegar

Put all the ingredients in a large saucepan and heat gently, stirring, until the sugar has dissolved. Raise the heat and simmer, stirring more often as it gets thicker.

When it passes the plate test*, ladle into clean half-pint and pint jars. Clean the jar rims and put on a lid and a rim. (I put the lids in a small saucepan and bring to a boil before using so the rubber seal is hot. There's a great magnetic tool to pick up the hot lids and deposit it on top of the jar.)

*Plate test: place a few saucers in the freezer. To test if the chutney is done, put a small bit of chutney on the plate and return to the freezer. Check in a minute or two. If there is not a lot of liquid around the chutney, it's thick enough and ready to can.

Process is a hot water bath for ten minutes.

Store in a cool, dark, dry place for one month before serving.

About Altars

I have always created altars in my home – in my bedroom, living room and even outside. I started by creating beauty and beautiful arrangements of loved items and candles. I did this for years before I realized they were altars. For me, it is a space to honor the beauty of life, and perhaps, both the seen and the unseen of life. Crystals, candles, flowers or plants and objects of importance to me are included. Found objects, too, like a beautiful leaf or a heart-shaped rock will get added. It is always evolving and changing – reflecting that I am, too.

I have found that when someone I love has passed, I am immediately drawn to create an altar space with photos of that loved one, with other mementos and flowers, and a candle or two or three. This provides a focus for me to honor them and to physically ground that I am holding them in my heart. It is a place and a space for remembrance. When my friend, Jane, who was like my second mother, died, I kept her altar for a year. With Mike, I moved my altar to different places. At first, his pictures and other items were on my bedroom altar – on top of a large chest of drawers – with candles and a statue of Ganesha I bought him in Bali. For the first few months, I also created an altar space in the living room. After this ceremony for the second anniversary of his death, I put the photos on a shelf in the changing area in my bedroom, a place I look at every day, and added miniature statues of

Indian Gods and Goddesses. This altar is still there. A place of my memories of Mike that I see every day.

When our cat, Clare, was put down, I printed out some photos of her and created an altar in the front hall – right in the center of the house – with flowers and a sculpture of a sleeping cat with wings I had found. Clare was sixteen years old and had been in our family for fourteen years. This was an important way for my daughter and me to acknowledge this sad passing in our lives. During this time, a friend died, and I put her photo on the altar with Clare. After a couple months, I moved the altar – with all the photos – to a new place in the living room. It didn't need to be the first thing we saw when we entered the house anymore. The sculpture of the sleeping cat with wings was eventually placed on her grave at my friend's house in the country.

Animals are as dear to us as our family and friends. It helps to acknowledge the grief by creating an altar to honor the place they held in the family.

The first cat I ever had was when I was given a kitten in the mid-1980's. I was living in Connecticut in the woods. I called him Rocky. He didn't like to be picked up but loved being petted. When he was a year old, he was run over. A neighbor found Rocky and buried him for me. I was devastated. I had no idea I would be so upset, so sad and grieving. Never having had pets growing up, I thought that saying, "I can't see you now, my cat just died" was overstating the situation. I was so totally wrong. I was heartbroken. Losing a cat – or dog – is losing a family member. Grieving an animal is the same as grieving a person. It's a heart connection, and it takes time to get over the change and the sadness.

I buried our cat, Thunder, just five months after we buried Clare. He was fifteen years old. The house was so quiet with him gone. Every day when I would come home, I would instinctively look for him and then remember that he was no longer here. He was such a sweet guy and had been my buddy following me around, keeping me company while I worked in the office or in the garden.

I made an altar for Thunder in the front hall so I could have a focus for remembering and mourning him. It was also to honor him for being part of our family and included pictures, his collar and a cat sculpture I purchased to eventually put on his grave.

My daughter was ten when she picked him out from three kittens neighbors left behind when they moved in the summer. We had an opening for a cat as our male cat, Hugger, was gone. She really wanted a black cat and there he was with big gold eyes. He got the cute kitten award at the vet when we took him in to get checked out. She named him Thunder. When the first rainstorm arrived late in the fall, he was out all night. He loved being in the rain. We knew he was not an ordinary cat. As he got older, we discovered he had what they call smoke fur – he looked like a black cat but with white on the inside half his fur.

It's funny that a critter that doesn't talk much would take up such a large space in my home and heart. I've found this with all my cats. I was surprised originally that cats were such wonderful company. After thirty-five years of cats, I decided to take a break to explore freedom without anyone at home I needed to take care of. It doesn't mean that I'm not sad that Thunder is gone. It is an ending and a beginning.

A Recipe for Altars

Creating an altar is actually simple. You can use the space on a bedroom dresser, a fireplace mantel, a table, or the top of a piano, for example. What you are creating is a space where you can focus your attention and your intention. It can be a special altar to remember a loved one or a favorite pet that has passed on, or an altar you create for a ceremony like I did for my husband's second anniversary. It is a way to remember someone or something from the past or to remind yourself of your desire in your life moving forward – or both.

As I look back over the decades, I have had an "always altar" somewhere in the house – way before I knew that they were called altars. I thought they were beautiful arrangements I could appreciate every time I looked at them. I never put anything on the altar except intentionally. It evolves and changes as the year goes by. Don't we all? My current bedroom altar started about twelve years ago when my husband, Mike, and I moved upstairs into our newly remodeled master bedroom furnished with his bedroom set including a lovely big wooden chest with many drawers. It called out to be the space for a bedroom altar. There are items that stay and others that get changed out. What stays is the carved wooden buddha with a very serene face that I got in Bali in the center of the altar, with a fragrant candle in a hand-blown glass container in front of buddha. The buddha reminds me that peace is present, and love is present – always. I have several crystal balls on the altar that I have collected over the years. There's a crystal cluster that my husband gave me for Christmas one year and a photo of my daughter and me.

There are also my two river rocks that fit together set on a little pedestal. Back in the early 70s, I was camping with friends on the North Fork of the Yuba River in Northern California. It was a hot summer day and my best friend, Kay, and I were standing knee deep in the rocky riverbed cooling off and chatting – about ten feet apart. We both reached down and picked up a rock. When we were back on the riverbank, we examined the rocks she and I had picked up and discovered they fit together. Over the fifty years we have been friends, we have taken turns having the rocks. For me, it is a reminder that there are no accidents. Life has a purpose and will show you the way – or provide a reminder that you ARE on the right path.

For me, altars are a place to create beauty and to be reminded of the beauty of life. I always have a plant or flowers on the altar. Lately, it's been a beautiful white orchid plant in a handsome cachepot. A cachepot is a decorative container without drainage that you place the plant in. It's usually ceramic but can be of any material. Crystals are reminders of the beauty of the natural world. Beauty is a high vibration and so are crystals. It takes a lot of pressure and time to create crystals in the earth.

In the book, *Real Life Rituals*, by Karyl Huntley, she defines altars as follows:

> "An altar is a physical site that has been designated as holy. It is a place where anyone may come to pray, meditate, ritualize, give thanks, receive blessing, or reflect on what is important and true. Although holiness is

everywhere, there seems to be a sense of the sacred at an altar. It can be a symbolic bridge between different worlds or states of being; between the spiritual world and the world of form, between the worlds of inner remembrance and outer awareness, between the state of confusion and the state of clarity.

"When you build your own altar, you assume that the same thing is happening - great holiness is revealed in your everyday life as blessing, clarity, connection, wisdom, inspiration, or spiritual support of some kind. Something important comes into your life from the world of possibility, and it is your altar that reminds you of this continuing miracle."

Essential ingredients for an altar:
Candle
Focal point – such as sculpture, vase of flowers, a group of candles
Favorite or memorable objects
Incense
Optional ingredients:
Found objects – leaf, rock, twig, pinecone, shell – many choices in the natural world
Photos
Inspirational Quotes

Altar Maintenance

Having an altar means you place attention on it. Sometimes more than other times. Keeping your altar clean and arranged – or rearranged as you see fit – as the days go by. Life keeps changing. Respect and honor the space you have made for beauty and connection. Consider grouping objects together, in groups of three or five. This gives the eye a place to land rather than having everything spread out evenly. You can have several groupings on an altar.

If you have young children, consider placing the altar higher than little hands can reach it. This is especially important if you have a candle burning. Children can also learn to honor and respect your altar. Perhaps they can add something they drew or made or found to the altar as a reflection of honoring them and their creativity.

Every so often I will move the furniture around in a room or make some decor changes to refresh the space. Changing the decor in a room, for me, is a reflection of the inner change that has occurred or is occurring in me. One of those changes may be to move my altar and re-create it in a new space with a new look and feel. Life keeps changing, so do my altars. Here's a progression of my altar over time.

Third Anniversary

October 21, 2012 was the third anniversary of Mike's death. It felt like a clearing, a time that I could now move forward and claim a new life for myself. I was ready to move away from so much remembrance and let go of the grief that would arise every so often. A woman friend I talked to told me that at year three after her husband's death she was ready to move on. I did a small ceremony for myself and for Mike in remembrance of him and his passing. I added flowers to my altar, lit a candle and meditated, giving thanks that Mike had been in my life.

Two weeks later came a phone call. My sister, Elizabeth, had fallen off a horse and was on her way to the emergency room. She was sixty and had been living in California for ten years. Elizabeth loved her weekly therapeutic horseback riding. She loved animals and had a special relationship with her horse. The horse had moved unexpectedly, and she fell off. I called my brother, and we met at the hospital ER. Elizabeth had broken six ribs. She had trouble breathing. They moved her from ER to the ICU. Trying to explain to Elizabeth that she needed to breathe deeply even though it really hurt was unsuccessful. She was not able to understand why she should bother to make the ball go up in the breathing test and she wasn't going to do it. In current terms, Elizabeth was developmentally disabled and had been diagnosed as being mentally about eleven years old. She could never be independent. She had lived at home with our father until age thirty when she moved to a wonderful group home outside Chicago called The Lambs. It was not until the mid-eighties that Elizabeth was diagnosed as having Prader-Willi Syndrome, a genetic disorder where one is constantly hungry and cannot control how much food they eat. Every calorie is double as their metabolism is so much slower. This explained why she had always been heavy, was short in stature and had developed diabetes – all common to this syndrome.

After 9/11, it seemed best to find a place in California for Elizabeth to be nearer my brother and me, rather than trying to connect long distance with her in Illinois. It took me a year to find a place. I found a Prader-Willi home about an hour away from us, which meant they provided specific meals and they locked the kitchen to insure no access. Being in this home allowed Elizabeth to gradually lose some weight. Around the time Elizabeth moved to CA, I was introduced to the owner and founder of Giant Steps Therapeutic Horseback Riding by a friend. Elizabeth loved animals, so riding a horse once a week was a thrill for her. It was sheer joy for her to be on her horse. Her blue eyes would light up sharing how she would tell her horse what to do and it would obey her. She was in charge on her horse. Not something she experienced in her everyday life.

She lived at the Prader-Willi home for about six years. The care in the home went downhill, unfortunately, and we had to find another place for her. I eventually found a wonderful place for her to live in Marin County just minutes away. It was the best living situation she had ever had with an organization called Lifehouse. Elizabeth continued to ride her horse once a week. Overall, she attended Giant Steps for about ten years.

I spent every day at the hospital checking in on Elizabeth and talking to the nurses. My brother was there just as often. We would tag team to be there with Elizabeth. After a week, they moved Elizabeth to just outside the ICU, to the Step-Down Unit. They kept Elizabeth on a breathing machine as she had trouble getting enough oxygen. The one day I was not there in the morning to check on her was the day they hadn't fed her or attended to her needs. I understood they were occupied with her roommate, but I was furious they had not taken care of her. I realized that being an advocate was so vital. Every day.

The hospital staff recommended she next be moved to a rehab hospital nearby. I went to see the rehab hospital and met some of the staff. Arrangements were made and Elizabeth was moved by ambulance. The doctor at the rehab hospital was wonderful and very attentive. Because Elizabeth had trouble breathing, she got pneumonia and from there it all went downhill. With the staff keeping her comfortable, Elizabeth passed peacefully – just three weeks after her fall from the horse. Both my brother and I were with her.

I called Elizabeth's house to let the staff know she had died and suggested we have a small memorial at the house in a week's time. I felt it was important for her roommates and the staff to have closure. Elizabeth's roommates and their families, the Lifehouse staff, the CEO of Lifehouse, the owners of Giant Steps and other good friends attended. They planted a tree in the backyard of the house. I invited everyone to write a quality about Elizabeth and tie it to the tree. We had a short ceremony. Both my brother and I spoke plus others shared experiences and memories of Elizabeth, especially noting her quick wit and humor. Food and beverages were served. The founder of Giant Steps said they would plant a tree at their facility. A couple months later, my brother and I took her ashes up to Giant Steps and scattered them around her tree and the stone with her name engraved on it at the base of the tree. It was so fitting to have her there near the horses.

I was now "relieved" of my duty as the older sister and mother for Elizabeth – which started when I was fourteen. I had had the responsibility and concern for her for over fifty years. In many ways she was much more a daughter than a sister. I was sad to see her go and found myself back in the groove of grieving. So much for moving on after Mike's death. Now I was again in this place of adjusting to the change. As the months went by, I would occasionally be out shopping and something would catch my eye and I would say to myself, "oh, that would be a good gift for Elizabeth," and then remember I didn't need to do that anymore.

I began to wonder what I wanted to do with the time that had opened up with this change, with this freedom from a long-time responsibility. I had had a desire to write a book about event planning, having taught it at Sonoma State University for four years, as well as teaching it to my clients. I hired a writing coach for the summer as I had no idea how to get started. In the fall, I took a class from a teacher, Leslie Keenan, who is a writer, editor and publisher. I learned so much. After I completed the class, I was invited to be in one of her writing groups that meets weekly to share what they have written and get feedback. I'm been in this writing group ever since. This book evolved out of my writing practice with the group's support and feedback. The event planning book is next.

Chapter Four
Return Journey

4 Years 5 months – Who's Counting?

March 13, 2014

I went to the bank today with a copy of Mike's death certificate. They needed the document as proof before being able to take his name off our joint bank account. I had forgotten all about this until I called the bank on an unrelated matter a couple days ago. When they looked up my account, they asked about the other name on my account. I had left Mike's name on the account after his passing until I had handled all the financial aspects. This took almost two years, and then I just forgot about it. It seemed like there was no reason now not to remove his name from our account. There it is again – our. I so miss that.

It was a simple and straightforward process to sign a new signature card and they took Mike's name off the account. I left the bank and found myself sad and teary. I was surprised at this bubbling up of sorrow within me. I guess this is a reminder that having his name removed from documents does not remove the love. That love connection is always present and does not fade or disappear. This was made palpably clear today. I still miss him . . . and, he is held in my heart.

Time to Discard My Widow's Weeds

September 21, 2014

I was in a meditation circle today and the last thing that came to me were the words, "discarding widow's weeds." The message was so clear I had to pay attention to it. I wondered what ARE widow's weeds? When I got home, I googled widow's weeds and found a book titled, *Widow's Weeds and Weeping Veils*, and ordered it.

I discovered that weed (waed) is Old English for garment. In Victorian times, a widow would wear mourning dress for two to four years. Queen Victoria led the example for what would be the Victorian style of mourning when her husband, Albert, died in 1861. She wore black for the rest of her life. When she died in 1901, the style of mourning slowly changed. Another reason they were called widow's weeds is that the lightweight black crepe fabric most often used to make the garments would fade after a lot of wear and look rather worn. There were many elaborate garments made in the style of the day in all black that were quite beautiful with lots of detail.

A month later, I discovered that The Costume Institute at the Metropolitan Museum of Art in New York opened an exhibit on October 21st called *Death Becomes Her, A Century of Mourning Attire 1815 to 1915*. The show exhibited clothes and accessories from this timeframe. Something was up with all this – at least for me!

There was etiquette and prescribed manners to mourning during that time. First, death was a common occurrence in the culture and was discussed openly. Death occurred most often in the home, not in a hospital. It was present in daily life. We have gotten so far away from this in today's world. There were signs that let everyone know a death had occurred – from putting black crepe on the front door, to the family dressed in black. There were specific rules to follow and even funeral foods served at home following the burial. Since the time for mourning was observed for years, the stages of mourning were expressed in the style and color of dress – from black to shades of grey and sometimes mauve. The recommended time for mourning differed for men, women and children and whether it was a spouse, child or relative that had died. Women had the primary responsibility for expressing the grief of the family through what they wore. Widows, especially, had to mourn longer and limit their social activities.

When I found out my husband had died, I thought . . . widow, I've never done that before. Even the word sounds strange. In our society today, we don't have the customs any more to recognize someone is grieving and to acknowledge that grieving takes time. It's not something one gets over and moves on in a speedy manner.

I really appreciate that the Jewish faith has a prescribed plan for death from the funeral very soon after the person has died, to sitting shiva for seven days and then another ceremony at the year's anniversary of the person's death. Sitting shiva means the mourners usually stay at home and receive guests to help them pray and reflect upon their loss. Shiva means seven. Marking time with ceremony – and support of friends and loved ones. It definitely helps the grieving process.

Who knew this process took so long. Now after five years, I am ready to move on and at the same time I find myself diving deeper into the past and learning about the culture of mourning we had a hundred years ago. Moving forward and going back. There is something for me to bring forward. It has yet to be revealed. Stay tuned.

Decorating for Christmas

December 10, 2014

Every year I take down the four large Christmas boxes from the attic and pull out treasured holiday decorations. I love fluffing up the whole house and arranging things differently each year. So many of the items are over twenty years old – from when my daughter was very little. Up went the stockings with the gold letters I ironed on spelling our names – with the backwards "D" in my name. Just the two stockings. It feels empty without both Mike's and my sister, Elizabeth's stockings. This is the second Christmas without Elizabeth and the fifth Christmas without Mike.

In decorating the house, I pulled out dishes and candles and linens and thought . . . I want to start having dinner parties again. It's been a long time. I mostly stopped entertaining since Mike died. I have had a few parties in the past five years, but not many. Mike and I would invite our friends over, and we would both cook. I'm ready to start cooking again for parties.

When my daughter was small, we would drive up to Petaluma, California, about thirty minutes north of our home, and cut down a Christmas tree. I cut down a tree every year for years. We would decorate the tree together. Santa would arrive during the night with presents surrounding the tree and stockings filled. I moved from cutting down a tree, to buying a live tree and using it for several years – as long as it would last. I would decorate the tree and leave it outside the large kitchen sliding door, bringing it in on Christmas Eve. Our annual Christmas morning tradition, after opening the gifts, is, as always, having a brunch of smoked salmon, bagels and cream cheese with capers, sliced red onions and lemon wedges, served with champagne or sparkling cider.

After Mike died, I didn't want to repeat our usual Christmas traditions. The first Christmas without Mike was just a week or so after his memorial in Marin, so we had Christmas at home. I was numb. The next year, my daughter and I did something different and went to Santa Fe for Christmas week. We enjoyed the traditions there, including their Christmas Eve Farolito Walk on Canyon Road with all the luminarias lining the walkway along the homes and shops. Farolito is Spanish for paper lantern. We thoroughly enjoyed our week there and took advantage of the hotel spa for massages.

This year, my daughter and I will have Christmas at home. Today, I've pulled down the four boxes and put out decorations around the house. It always makes me think of my friend, Jane, who was like a second mother to me in high school and beyond. She would decorate the house from top to bottom on December 1st. I try to make that December 1st deadline, although it is more likely I get to it just a little later in the month. Christmas will be a leisurely morning opening our stockings, the gifts around the tree and then our classic Christmas brunch. Later in the day, we will join my brother and sister-in-law at their home for Christmas dinner and exchange gifts. It's relaxed and low-key day. Just the way I like it.

Stormy Soup Day

December 11, 2014

I hunkered down for a storm day (predicted huge winds/rain/flooding) with meetings cancelled and made celery soup in the kitchen listening to the steady heavy rain. The sound of the rain feels so good after three years of drought – it's music to cook by.

I'm going to a holiday party with friends tomorrow night and need to bring something. Since I had the celery from my garden, I decided to make soup to pass as an hors d'oeuvre served in small cups. I planted the celery with the intention of making celery salt, which I made. I had made it last year and wanted more.

Harvesting the celery – and the parsley and basil became the inspiration for what to make. Make something with what you've got – that seems to be the rule of the garden. Since I used all the celery leaves with the sea salt, I was left with all the stems. I simmered the celery with onion, leek, celery root, potato and roasted cauliflower, then pureed with an immersion blender and finished it with some coconut milk and parsley pesto. I turned the herb harvest from the garden into several kinds of pesto – basil parsley pesto, arugula parsley pesto and parsley pesto. There was a lot of parsley.

Make something with what you've got. That's a rule for life, too, it seems. What shows up is what you've got – and now what do you do with it? Widow was something I got. Written that way, it sounds like a disease. It was a dis-ease, for sure. Not ease. Not easy. I didn't plan it, but it showed up. The harvest seems to be reflecting and writing about my experience, process and feelings of being a widow. Widow still sounds like a weird word. Now I want to make something else. I feel like I've done widow. Time to move on.

Celery Soup

Ingredients:

    1 lb fresh celery
    1 celery root
    1 medium Russet or other starchy potato
    2 Tbsp EVOO
    1 medium onion, peeled and roughly chopped
    1 to 2 leeks, white part cleaned and sliced
    1 clove garlic, peeled and chopped
    ½ cup dry white wine
    1 qt vegetable stock or chicken stock
    1 cup coconut milk or coconut cream
    Roasted cauliflower (optional)
    Kosher salt, to taste
    Ground pepper, to taste

Preparation:

1. Slice celery into ½-inch pieces. Don't worry about precision as the soup will be puréed. You want the pieces to be of uniform size, so they cook evenly.

2. Peel the potato and cut it into 1-inch cubes/pieces.

3. In a heavy-bottomed soup pot, heat the olive oil over medium heat.

4. Add the onion and leek. Cook for 5 minutes or so, until the onion is slightly translucent.

5. Add the garlic and celery and cook for another 4-5 minutes.

6. Add the wine and cook for a couple minutes on high heat until the wine is reduced by half.

7. Add the vegetable or chicken stock and the potato. Increase the heat to medium-high and bring to a boil. Then lower the heat and simmer for 15-20 minutes until the celery and potatoes are soft enough that they can easily be pierced with a knife.

8. Remove from heat and puree the soup using an immersion blender. If you use a blender, puree the soup in small batches – and be careful, hot soup in a blender can zoom to the ceiling! The steam will blow the lid off! Best to let it cool first if using a blender.

9. Return puréed soup to pot and bring to a simmer again, adding more stock to adjust the thickness if necessary. When the soup is ready, I add about 1 cup of coconut cream and let the soup heat up again.

10. Season to taste with salt and pepper and serve in bowls or mugs. If you've made the pesto, add some just before serving, stirring it well into the soup. It's not necessary, I've made and served the soup without it to raves. It just adds another element.

Optional – Before you get started with the soup, cut the cauliflower into small florets. Make them about the same size so all roast evenly. Toss with olive oil, salt & pepper and spread in a rimmed baking sheet. Roast at 400 degrees for about 20 minutes. I love this as a side dish. I had leftovers of roasted cauliflower that I added to the soup before I pureed it.

Makes about 1½ quarts (6 8-oz. servings) of soup.

Pesto recipes

Arugula Parsley Pesto
 2 garlic cloves
 2 cups arugula
 2 cups parsley
 1/3 cup pine nuts, toasted
 1/2 cup grated parmesan cheese
 1/2 teaspoon salt
 Juice of 1 lemon
 1/4 cup olive or grapeseed oil
 1/4 cup hot water, if needed

Clean and remove stems from arugula and parsley. In food processor, chop garlic first. Then add arugula, parsley, nuts, parmesan, lemon juice and process. With processor on, add oil and then hot water. Add salt to taste.

Note: I prefer grapeseed oil as it is light and does not overpower the flavor of the greens.

Makes about two cups, 16 ounces.

Variations

Basil Parsley Pesto
 Substitute basil for arugula

Options for nuts – substitute toasted pepitas for pine nuts

Do not add hot water, only grapeseed or olive oil

Parsley Pesto

4 cups parsley – no basil or arugula

Options for nuts – substitute toasted pepitas or walnuts for pine nuts

Do not add hot water, only grapeseed or olive oil

Chapter Five
On Track

Landing in New York

January 17, 2015

I am about to land at JFK airport in New York. I haven't been here in over eleven years. So much has happened in my life in that time. As we touched down at JFK, I thought, I am a different person than I was then. I got married, became a widow, my daughter grew from a young teen to a young woman, and now I'm landing in New York to bring some further closure and exploration to mourning and death. I never suspected this would be the reason to get me back to New York. The last time I was here was with my daughter for my cousin's memorial – another time of loss and grieving. I hadn't had the perspective of thinking about the last ten to eleven years as a chunk of time to compare before now. I am discovering that place has memories, or more accurately that it allows buried memories to bubble up into awareness.

Mourning Research

January 20, 2015

Yesterday I visited the Costume Institute exhibit at the Metropolitan Museum in New York called *Death Becomes Her, A Century of Mourning Attire*. The clothes were amazing – such detail in black garments reflecting the fashion of different ages from 1815 to 1915. It also reflected the etiquette of mourning and what was required – most specifically for women, as they bore the most responsibility for visibly expressing the mourning and grief for their whole family – and reflecting their social standing and "level of respectability." Sometimes children would wear white instead of black – the absence of color – with black trim.

I didn't know that wearing black to represent mourning dates all the way back to the late Middle Ages. In the 1800s, the rules of mourning etiquette were very prescribed. The periods for what to wear were divided into stages from "unrelieved black" for first-stage mourning moving to black and white, or gray and mauve, which reflected the "easing of one's grief" – moving from heavy morning to middle mourning to lighter mourning. How long the periods lasted depended upon the relationship of the deceased to the mourners. Deepest mourning was worn by a widow for her husband for at least two to four years. The mourning of a father or mother worn for one year, and for a brother or sister for six months. Just putting on the black garments reminded those of why they were doing so – as "tangible evidence of the reality of their husband's or family member's passing, a way to accept the death, to keep the memory alive, as well as working through one's grief."

As fashions evolved, mourning attire reflected these fashion changes. Widow's mourning attire in Europe and America was "rooted in monastic dress of the Middle Ages, of the habits of nuns being emblematic of the modesty and chastity that widow's mourning should signal as a renunciation of worldly allure." Queen Victoria was so devastated by the death of her husband, Prince Albert, in 1861 that she entered deep mourning and wore widow's black clothing until her death in January 1901. It was also a huge blow to everyone in the country. There were many riding a special train to down to London for the Prince's funeral. One woman was quoted as saying, "We were all in deep mourning and the ladies wore crepe veils like widows." That was literally a grief train. This quote reminded me of seeing Jacqueline Kennedy wearing a black veil for the funeral of her husband, John F. Kennedy, which was not something I saw in the 1960s. It seems it might have been a reflection of the formality of the ceremony of that sad day and the position of JFK as President of the United States.

At least in the past, there was recognition through clothing when someone was in mourning. Now, it's difficult to know if this is the case and we seem impatient for someone to move along. A friend I know wore black for two years after her husband died. She did it for herself, for her own mourning.

I never felt I needed to wear black. A friend asked me what I wore to Mike's Memorial. I did not remember and had to watch the video recording to see. I wore a lime green cashmere top with a long black silk skirt. I wanted some color, something bright in the dark and not the heaviness of all black. Yes, we were mourning Mike at the Memorial, and we were also celebrating his life.

Here are some photos from the exhibit, Death Becomes Her, A Century of Mourning Attire 1815 – 1915:

According to family history, Amelia Jane Carley (1844–1892) wore this dress at her marriage to William Edward Chess (1842–1926) in 1868 in West Virginia, the half-mourning colors chosen in honor of those who died during the Civil War. Both bride and groom were fortunate not to have lost any immediate family during the war, though Ms. Carley's brother and Mr. Chess served in the Union Army. This family narrative suggests that the bride chose shades of mourning in response to the widespread losses suffered during the war rather than to memorialize an individual. A subdued palette of gray and black may have felt more respectful than a showier bridal gown while so many families still grieved. Etiquette manuals and women's magazines frequently offered guidance for brides whose weddings intersected with a period of mourning, though the choice of dress under such circumstances often reflected a woman's personal judgment rather than prescriptive advice.

Sheryl Sandberg and All of Us

June 10, 2015

When Sheryl Sandberg posted June 3rd on Facebook about her thirty days of mourning since her husband died, it pulled me into her deep feelings and grief. I so related to what she said. Although I have not been posting for quite a while, I have written more about the loss of my husband as well as exploring grief in our society.

Sheryl so eloquently shares her thoughts and feelings – allowing others to remember and share those same feelings of grief even if they hadn't expressed it as well as Sheryl has. I am in tears each time I read it. She also shares how to relate to those in mourning from her own thirty-day perspective. Most people don't know what to say. Sheryl writes: "Real empathy is sometimes not insisting that it will be okay but acknowledging that it is not." Or, just changing the question by adding "today" – "How are you today?" Simple yet subtle shifts for greater connection and understanding.

I am grateful that she shared her feelings with the world. It seems to me that death, grieving and mourning are coming out of the shadows in some ways. It affects us all. Sheryl's post going viral reflects a connection and readiness to receive this depth of sharing about something common to all of us. Her post made the front page of the *San Francisco Chronicle* the next day.

Each week, there seems to be an Op-Ed article in the Sunday New York Times that addresses death and grieving. I see these articles as a further opening of this conversation in our society.

Why Do We Send Flowers?

December 11, 2015

I recently planned and coordinated a Memorial for a client. In two weeks, I helped her decide who was speaking and what was to be included in the service, and what photos, quote and song were to be printed in the program.

I made cards (8.5×5.5) for the guests to write a note to her and her son in place of a guest book.

Many friends donated food and one made beautiful floral arrangements that included white lilies, her husband's favorite flower. After the Memorial, I insisted she take the flowers home. I put the two large arrangements in her car to make sure she took them home. Two days later she texted me, "you were right about the flowers."

She was referring to my first blog post when I had sent her the link to my widowz healing blog (that's what I called it when I started it) a few days before the memorial. When she couldn't sleep, she read all the posts. I hoped this meant that she felt the love and support of those that were present at the memorial – and that it also represented the love her husband had for her and her son. About a week later I asked her what she discovered about the flowers. She said, "I am happy to have them, but I also see their impermanence - just like life."

In a recent Sunday *New York Times* "Modern Love" column, this paragraph jumped out at me:

"Why do we send flowers? To make up for what is intangible? Those feelings we can't hold in our hands and present as a gift to our loved ones? And why is it that the placeholders we choose – the dozen red roses, the fragrant white lilies, the long-stemmed French tulips – are so fleeting? Hold on to them for too long and you end up with a mess of petals, pollen and foul-smelling water."

The article was about working in a flower shop, the stories people share when they buy flowers, and the variety of messages on the accompanying cards. This note was unusually honest: 'Cards and flowers seem so lame when someone dies but we are thinking of you and want you to know.'

This definitely says what is true. We want to send our love and heart-felt caring to friends and family when they experience the loss of a loved one and; it IS hard to know what to say. Flowers say it for us, though not usually with such a direct message included. For me, the beauty of flowers also represents the beauty of life. They are alive, beautiful and ephemeral – a reminder to honor the preciousness of life in each and every moment.

Is it Grief or Loss . . . or Both?

January 10, 2016

In an article in the *New York Times*, "The Smell of Loss," the author Julie Myerson describes her experiences smelling her mother-in-law's perfume a year or more after she had died. Her exploration of why the scent persists at times includes asking scientists and others for their explanation of this phenomenon. It's a hallucination, a ghost, or the brain's way of bringing up a memory – a sensory memory, they say.

I had a similar experience of scent about a month after my husband died. I came upstairs to our bedroom and there was the very strong smell of coffee. He drank coffee every morning. There was no coffee made or being made in the kitchen downstairs. The smell was unmistakably coffee. I did not go searching for where that scent was coming from. I figured he had shown up to say hello. I had not gone searching for why this occurred. After reading this *New York Times* article, I googled "smelling perfume of deceased." The first site I found listed the "Top Ten Signs from your Loved Ones in Spirit." Turns out I'd had several of these common experiences. I also checked out the site from the authors of *Hello From Heaven*. They call them ADC's – After Death Communications. They had done similar research.

In my Internet search, I learned that the ability to smell the fragrance from a deceased loved one is called clairgustance. Hearing a voice is called clairaudience. Getting a phone call is also common. I got that one. I wished I'd saved it. There was a message on my cell phone that just said, "I love you" – very softly. I knew it was from my husband. I received the message the day after he died. Another common experience is receiving a physical sign. I had a friend tell me there were a lot of butterflies after their father's funeral. I think my husband showed up as a raccoon in my backyard after his memorial. I didn't say that my best friend did. The raccoon just stared and stared at us. A friend's mother had an owl that visited her every day for a week after her husband died.

Another sign is movement such as a photo or picture falling off the wall, or an object is moved. I had that one, too. I gave my husband a small metal heart after we were married, and he always carried it in his pocket with his change. I had put in on the altar I created on our bedroom dresser. One day I discovered it had been moved, and it wasn't by me or anyone else. Strange electrical occurrences such as lights or appliances going on or off, or clocks stopping are other signs. Another is that we might hear buzzing noises in our ears. I read that they are communicating from a higher frequency, which may be experienced as ringing or buzzing in our ears. I hadn't thought about that one being applicable, and I don't think it is for me. I had some buzzing in my ears that got more pronounced after the Elton John concert I attended this summer.

A friend of mine's husband visited her every night, turning on the TV in the middle of the night. She checked the remote and found it was set to go on at 3:00 am. She turned that setting off and still the TV turned on in the middle of the night. After a couple weeks it subsided. Then he would turn on the TV for milestones – on his birthday, when their cat died. At the fourth anniversary of his death, he showed up again by turning on the TV in the middle of the night. The last time he showed up, she had come early from work, in the mid-afternoon, and the TV was on, which had never happened before. She decided to sit down in front of the TV and talk to him. There was a green stripe on the screen that started to have pulses like he was talking. She told him she was happy that he was here, that she loved him. In the "conversation," she felt he was happy she had found a new partner. Her husband had also made his presence known at his memorial outdoors in a beautiful redwood grove. The chaplain had spoken, a friend got up and spoke and then another friend got up with his guitar and sang a song, Leonard Cohen's "Anthem." When he got to "There's a crack, a crack in everything" – everyone heard an intense cracking sound as a tree snapped in half and fell over by the creek nearby. Everyone stopped. Then he finished the phrase, "That's how the light gets in" and completed the song.

Overall, from what I have read and experienced myself, I believe these experiences are real and they are not hallucinations. So many people have had these experiences. And sometimes the inexplicable is just that. I'm ok with that. Are you?

The crux is that grief is a process that takes time and we get signs to help us along – from life as well as sometimes from the deceased. The change from having that person we love at hand and then gone is the hardest part to adjust to. As the author Julie Myerson quotes in her article, "Loss. Isn't that the hardest lesson of human existence? The finality of losing someone you love, of having them fall right out of your life forever: the cold and terrible permanence of it."

And yet, I have discovered that what lives on is the love. The love never dies or is lost. We hold it in our heart always. When we experience a loss, our heart is cracked open. And just like Leonard Cohen says: "That's how the light gets in."

The Grief Train

January 28, 2016

"Bereavement. Or, Bereaved. Bereft. It's from the Old English bereafian, meaning 'to deprive of, take away, seize, rob'." This quote is from *H is for Hawk* by Helen McDonald. If you look up the word in the dictionary, bereavement means a period of mourning after a loss, especially after the death of a loved one; a state of intense grief. Another definition a little closer to the origin of the word is "the condition of having been deprived of something or someone valued, especially through death." Today, I think we refer to bereavement as a time of mourning, although both are true. There's no rushing it. It takes years, really. It has its own schedule.

The grief train doesn't have a schedule. It can show up any time and surprise us. That wave of grief requires us to feel our feelings when it arrives at our station.

We are mourning for being deprived of our loved one, being robbed of that person in our life. They are taken away and we don't see them again. They aren't available to talk to, to spend time with anymore. That's the hard part, the hurt part, and it takes time to heal or at least to feel less tender about the loss. It's not something that can be analyzed or thought through, it touches our heart, our emotion. Emotion is energy in motion, like waves on the ocean. We can't control the waves and we can't control the waves of emotion.

Sometimes, when I think of my friend, Jane, the neighbor I met in high school who became like a second mother, and who has been gone for many years now, the grief train arrives at my station and I am brought to tears – missing her. I grieve the unconditional love that she had for me that was so precious. I learned what unconditional love is from her.

Helen McDonald says in another place in her book, "Sometimes I felt I was living in a house at the bottom of the sea." Grief requires diving deep into those waves and sitting in the midst of those feelings. We cannot rise back up to the living without first getting to the bottom of our emotions and grief.

Bereavement is a station I can be residing in, or not even notice I am still there after so long . . . and surprise, the grief train will stop at my station. I believe the work is to be willing to greet that train, to honor and acknowledge it, and sit with it when it arrives.

For more about grief and the difference between grief and sadness, see Karla McLaren's book, The Language of Emotions.

In Summary

I am in a totally different place than I was when I started my widowz healing blog in 2010 after Mike's death. I was in shock and grief at that time. The process of putting my blog together in a book form brought up a lot of grief and strong feelings at first; however, by the end of this journey, the strong emotions don't wash over me and stop at my station much anymore. I was asked, "How do you let go of grief and still hold that person close to you?" I don't think there's a letting go as much as time heals and changes the experience. I moved from the fog of grief to less fog, still immersed in mourning to a clearer presence and awareness of grief that over time just occasionally washed over me. The truth is . . . the love always remains.

I knew Mike for six years. It seems like it was longer than that. Even though I lost him, I realize that the time we had together was a gift. I feel blessed to have had him in my life. I hope that I have honored his memory and our memories together. As I now close this book and this chapter in my life, I am ready for whatever new adventures are in store for me. My intention is to keep learning, growing and expressing joy and love in this experience we call Life. I wish this for you, as well.

Acknowledgements

The web of life connects us all and there are more people than I can thank by name on this page. Nevertheless, I must make an attempt.

First, I must thank my writing group without whose encouragement to turn my blog posts into a book, I never would have done so. My great appreciation to the unwavering support of our leader and teacher, Leslie Keenan, and to Christine Mann, Jennifer Kloeping, Madeline Mendelson, Janis Rader, Cathy Rath, and Veronica Smith.

Huge gratitude for all my friends that said yes and pre-ordered a book (or multiple copies) that helped me launch the process of getting this book published, especially these very generous supporters Janet Craddock, Kim Erixon, Deborah Erwin, Hunter Freeman, Esther Follett, Dale Johnston, Morgan Hall, Phil Hallstein, Matthew Lombardi, John Miller, Judy Miller, Frank Paré, Yvonne Roberts, Sharon Wultich, and David Young. Woohoo to all!

Special thanks to my dear friends, my family and my tribe.

Lastly, to my publisher – great appreciation for seeing the potential in my book and giving me a hand up to print the book to then be able to help many others that have experienced love and loss.

About the Author

Marinda Freeman is a life-long spiritual student of many religions and disciplines and has been a spiritual counselor and teacher for 20 years. Her successful event design business for 30 years offers planning and production services to corporations, businesses, organizations and individuals. Marinda teaches classes and writes articles about the principals of event design as the foundation for beautiful and successful events. She is passionate about building community and connection – the real purpose of any event.

Note from the Author

Word of mouth is crucial for any author to succeed. If you enjoyed *The Grief Train*, please leave a review online—anywhere you are able. Even if it's just a sentence or two. It would make all the difference and would be very much appreciated.

Thanks!
Marinda

Thank you so much for reading
one of our **Memoir/Grief** novels.
If you enjoyed the experience, please check out our
recommendation for your next great read!

Blue Yarn by Carrie Classon

"...a reminder that we all are adventurers and must
follow our paths to wherever they might lead... a joy to
read." – *The Paris News*

View other Black Rose Writing titles at
<u>www.blackrosewriting.com/books</u> and use promo code
PRINT to receive a **20% discount** when purchasing.